LAST MINUTE DINNER PARTY

Frankie Unsworth

Photography Lisa Linder

LAST MINUTE

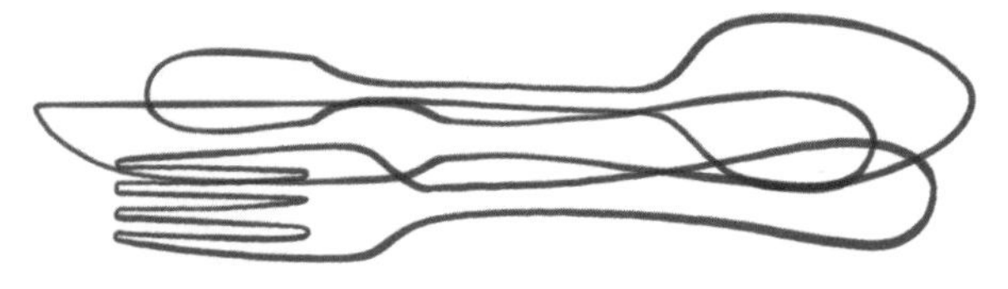

DINNER PARTY

Hardie Grant

NORTH AMERICA

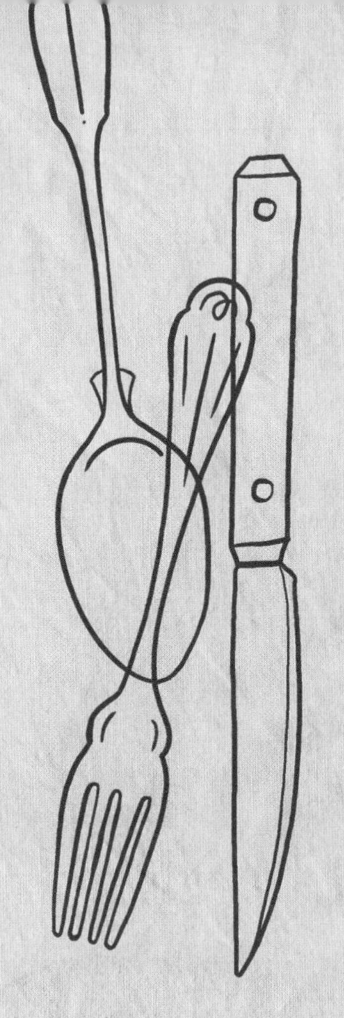

CONTENTS

WELCOME 06
DRINKS & NIBBLES 16
APPETIZERS 46
ON THE TABLE IN 20 66
PASTA & NOODLES 84
SHEET PAN & ONE POT 110
A LITTLE FANCIER 130
DESSERTS 154
MAKE AHEAD 184
MENU PLANNERS 200

WELCOME

So many of us love to have friends over, but too often social occasions turn into fussy affairs, leaving you frazzled before the first guest appears. This book is here to offer a hassle-free approach to entertaining, championing simplicity in favor of showiness, from quick post-work dinners all cooked in one pan to deceptively simple show-stopping suppers for a Friday night with friends. I want to show you how having a handful of useful, tasty, and simple recipes can revolutionize your approach to entertaining impromptu guests.

With shortcuts and make-ahead tips from a very busy cook on how to pull off the perfect carefree dinner for friends, through to simple get-ahead recipes to batch cook at the weekend, and freezer shortcuts, this book is here to remove the stress of cooking for a small crowd.

Last Minute Dinner Party is about creating delicious food by shopping sensibly, stocking your pantry with the essentials, and making them the building blocks of your cooking. Many of the recipes can be made from pantry ingredients, while others use made-ahead elements, freezer stocks, and fewer fresh ingredients than you can count on one hand.

Once you have perfected the get-ahead larder, there's no need to plan ahead on a daily basis to be sure to have a delicious dinner at the ready, whether it's an ancho chile-spiked base for a spicy acqua pazza or a deeply satisfying dukkah-spiced sheet pan schnitzel.

Lengthy ingredient lists in most cookbooks can be intimidating, difficult to source, and expensive, but this book offers inspiration for an impromptu evening meal using the most basic of ingredients, while suggesting the odd fresh ingredient to pimp it up.

Once you start combining these pantry perennials with the occasional visit to the butcher, fish supplier, or the grocery store, you'll discover a new way to cook and shop, waste less food, save time, and entertain friends at home without so much as breaking a sweat.

KEY TO SYMBOLS

 DRINKS  VEGAN  DAIRY FREE  NUT FREE

 NIBBLES  VEGETARIAN  GLUTEN FREE

PANTRY STAPLES

As a food stylist and recipe developer, I admit my pantry is more extravagantly stocked than the average cook's, but Iranian pistachios or nibbed sugar aren't necessarily the things I turn to when I need to create a "last minute dinner party." Keeping a well-stocked pantry containing some favorite ingredients, is one of the cornerstones of this book. My pantry includes easy-to-find flavor enhancers that will elevate your dishes, along with the best jarred vegetables to have on hand for fresh flavors that don't depend on a trip to the grocery store.

Kimchi, pickles, sauerkraut
Ferments are not only great for gut bacteria, but they add a big punch of acidity and tang to dishes that don't have fresh ingredients. I like to use kimchi for a crunch and an umami hit.

Dried spices (ground and whole), herbs, chiles, hibiscus, seeds, nuts
Store spices like ground and whole cumin seeds, ground and whole coriander, and turmeric to hand, as well as dried chiles (ancho) and a good store of nuts, such as pine nuts and walnuts.

Flavor-packed pastes
Tamarind, harissa, chipotle paste, gochujang, and miso paste are all important in my culinary repertoire; a spoonful here and there goes a very long way in lifting a dish.

Whole roasted peppers, jarred artichokes, sundried tomatoes, olives, capers
Whether you want to conjure up a quick antipasto plate or add a vegetable element to a dish like the Chicken-Kinda Cacciatore (page 128), a stash of preserved vegetables can be the perfect stand-in for fresh. Opt for jarred versus canned.

Sweet jams, savory chili jam, caramelized onion jam/relish mustards, vinegars
I use both wholegrain and Dijon mustards extensively for dressings.

Panko breadcrumbs
These Japanese breadcrumbs are light and airy and store in a jar indefinitely. I use them to add a quick crunch and crispiness.

Jarred/canned beans and legumes, quick-cook rice or lentil pouches
If the bean or legume is the hero of the dish I tend to favor jarred ones as they have a much better flavor and texture. Packs of precooked lentils and grain mixes are also very useful.

Canned fish
Canned fish has certainly made a hipster comeback thanks to a wide variety of great quality products with very cool packaging.

Coconut milk, canned tomatoes, stocks
Add coconut milk to Asian-inspired curries, dhals, and broths, and always have a store of canned tomatoes, bouillon cubes, or long-life stock.

Noodles and pasta
Goes without saying that noodles and pasta are essentials for the last minute pantry.

Oils and vinegars
I use olive, canola, and sesame oils most frequently, as well as sherry vinegar, white and red vinegar, rice vinegar, mirin, soy, and a good-quality extra-virgin olive oil for drizzling.

CHILLED ESSENTIALS

These are my refrigerator essentials—my most versatile ingredients to keep in stock for easy entertaining. My approach focuses on prioritizing a few long-life vegetables, such as onions, garlic, and potatoes, and a few little tricks for prolonging the life of more delicate herbs and leaves. Vegetables aside, these are my go-to refrigerator basics, to have on hand to make most of the recipes in this book, from tofu and eggs through to sour cream and Parmesan.

Onions, shallots, and garlic

Although not technically stored in the refrigerator (a cool dark place is ideal), these are an essential base flavor to numerous dishes, from stocks and stews to stand-alone dishes.

Cabbage, Tuscan kale, chard, broccoli rabe

The sturdier your leafy green, the longer they will keep. Wrap in damp cloth bags in the refrigerator—the moisture keeps them fresh and the protective layer stops them drooping.

Root vegetables

Winter squash, vacuum-packed cooked beet, potatoes, raw beet, and carrots. If you find carrots or beets have gone soft, put them into a bath of ice water for 15 minutes and they will perk up.

Herbs

Fresh herbs aren't the easiest items to store, so having some in the freezer is excellent, but for prolonging the life of a bunch of soft herbs, like cilantro, pluck off the leaves, wash them, then spin-dry in a salad spinner. Drain and store in the spinner. If storing a whole bunch, put them stem down into a jar with a few inches of water, cover with a bag, and store in the refrigerator door.

Salad leaves

You'll notice a fondness for bitter leaves weaving their way into the dishes in this book. Heads of radicchio and other bitter leaves keep longer than baby salad leaves. Wrap in damp cloth bags in the refrigerator. The method for the herbs also works well with tender leaves.

Eggs

As long-lasting as a protein gets, eggs are an essential in my refrigerator. They will last beyond their expiration date for 2 to 3 weeks.

Gnocchi and ravioli

Stored in the refrigerator or freezer, these are handy for last minute dinner parties.

Tofu, paneer, and cheeses

While hard cheeses will last well in the freezer, soft cheeses such as goat cheese, ricotta, and burrata are a freezer no-no. Most cheeses, even very fresh ones, will last a week in the refrigerator.

Dairy such as yogurt, heavy cream, milk, crème fraîche

I always have a few dairy items on the go as a spoonful here and there really elevates a dish. I also turn to them for a quick dessert.

Meat and fish

I buy meat and fish when I know what I am cooking to be sure I am eating it fresh and not wasting anything, but a pack of pancetta is useful to add to the shopping list and keeps well.

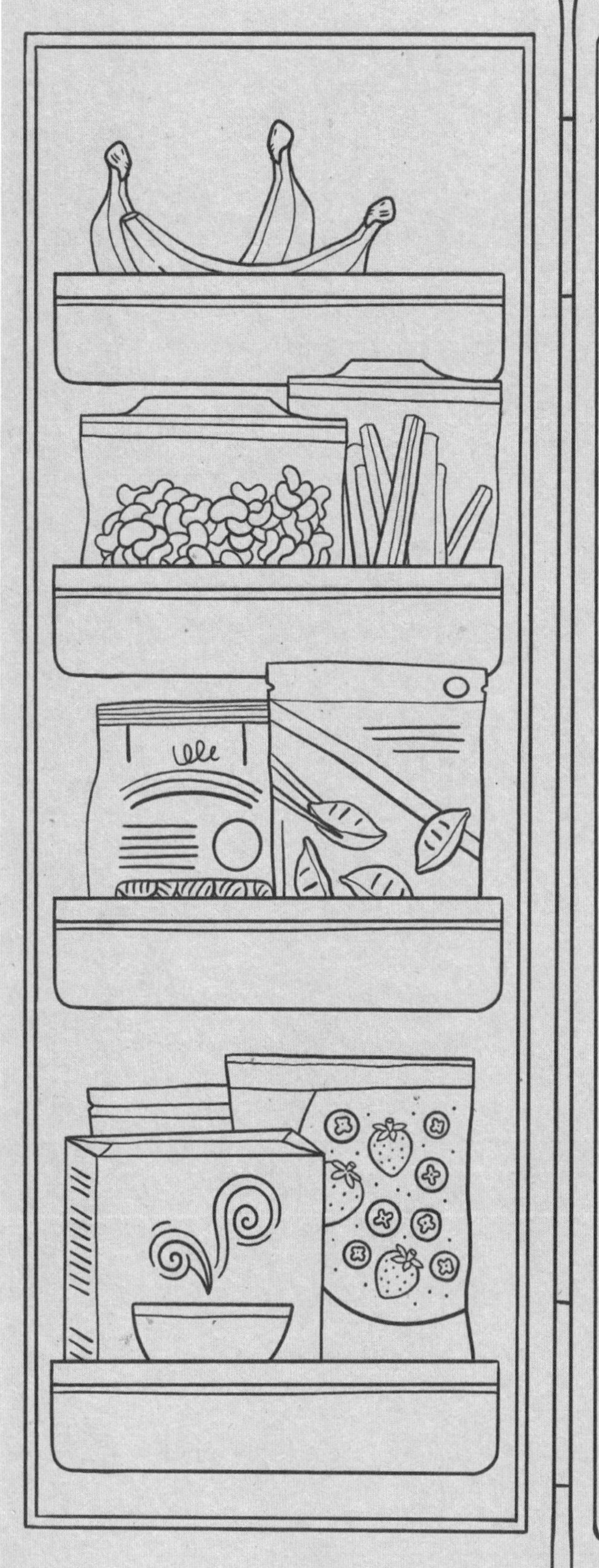

FREEZER ESSENTIALS

In my kitchen the freezer is almost as essential as the stove and oven when it comes to cooking for an impromptu dinner party. It plays host to all those ingredients that might have gone to waste, and houses the stocks and spice pastes (page 190) I've batch prepared at the weekend. Most items will keep for at least 3 months in the freezer. Make the freezer your friend and you'll never be too far from a good meal.

Fruits
Frozen berries, cherries, mango, banana, and citrus all freeze well, and while they aren't the same as fresh for eating, in their frozen form they can add a great deal more, like the Mango fro-yo (page 180) that whizzes up into an instant sorbet.

Gnocchi, noodles, wontons, and gyoza
These all freeze well and can be used straight from frozen. Keep a stock of these and you'll never be too far from a good dinner.

Pastry—puff, shortcrust, phyllo
These all store well in the freezer. Be sure to remove from the freezer and defrost in the refrigerator for 6 to 8 hours, or leave at room temperature for 1 to 2 hours before using. Make sure it is well sealed, otherwise it will dry out.

Vegetables
I like to always have chiles, garlic, ginger, lemongrass, whole leaf spinach, peas, broccoli, corn, and edamame in the freezer.

Herbs and herb cubes
You can freeze whole herbs in baking parchment-lined layers in the freezer or make ice cubes from chopped ones. Chop well-washed herbs, pack them tightly into ice-cube trays, add enough water to cover, and freeze.

Stock, gravy, wine cubes, and lemon juice cubes
I divide up my stock into 1 or 2 freezer proof containers so that I don't need to defrost it all. I also pour leftover wine into ice-cube trays to freeze. These small amounts can then be dropped into a recipe as and when it's required.

Ice cream
Freeze scoops of ice cream on a baking sheet, which can then be pepped up with some candied citrus peel (page 199) for a simple dessert.

Cheese/grated cheeses
Grate leftover pieces of cheese and freeze in bags. Hard cheeses work well, and once grated, will defrost quickly. Store for up to 3 months.

Precooked legumes and beans
These are more delicious than canned. Follow package directions on cook times, then store cooked and drained in freezer bags.

Shrimp and breaded fish fillets
Some fish is made to freeze, and shrimp and breaded fish are among my favorite standbys.

Bread/breadcrumbs
Blitz a couple-of-days'-old bread in a food processor then freeze it in a bag. Slice and freeze whole fresh loaves for speedy bruschetta.

DRINKS & NIBBLES

5-MINUTE CRISPY ROSEMARY & SEA SALT FARINATA

SERVES : 2 TO 4 AS A SNACK
PREP TIME : 5 MINS
COOK TIME : 5 MINS

½ cup (65g) chickpea flour
Extra-virgin olive oil, for cooking
2 bushy rosemary sprigs, leaves picked
Flaky sea salt

I have been making a variation of this recipe for over 2 decades, and I've yet to find a more satisfying canapé to serve with drinks than this one. If you have a couple of onions, scallions, or shallots, finely slice them and add at the same time as the rosemary.

Place the chickpea flour in a large bowl, pour in ½ cup (120ml) water, and whisk until smooth.

Heat a 10½-inch (26-cm) cast-iron skillet over high heat. Cover the base of the pan with a good layer of oil. When it's hot, add the batter and swirl to cover the bottom, the edges should sizzle and get really crispy. Sprinkle with plenty of salt and the rosemary leaves, then cook for 2 to 3 minutes until the edges are golden and sizzled. Flip over and cook for another 1 minute.

Cut the farinata into triangles and serve at once.

BLOODY MARY STATION

SERVES : 4
PREP TIME : 5 MINS

64 ounces (1.9 liters) tomato juice
25 ounces (750ml) vodka
12 ounces (350ml) Tabasco sauce
10 ounces (300ml) Worcestershire sauce
4 lemons, cut into wedges
Celery salt, for sprinkling
8 green pitted olives
8 pickled guindilla peppers
8 cherry tomatoes
8 celery stalks
Black pepper

The beauty of a Bloody Mary station is that not only are your guests customizing their own drink to their particular taste, but it encourages them to help themselves, leaving you to finish cooking dinner. Use your best tray and nicest highballs, then fill an ice bucket with plenty of ice and you are good to go. I also like to include a few toothpicks to allow people to make their own garnish with the olives, tomatoes, and pickled guindilla peppers.

As a general guideline, fill a large pitcher with the tomato juice over plenty of ice. For each glass, add 2 ounces (60ml) of vodka, and top off with the tomato juice. Add 3 to 4 shakes of Tabasco and Worcestershire sauces, and a generous squeeze of lemon juice. Sprinkle with celery salt and a grind of black pepper.

Skewer an olive, pickled guindilla pepper, and a cherry tomato onto a toothpick. Add a celery stalk to the glass and enjoy.

TABASCO

GILDA PINXTO

MAKES : 12
PREP TIME : 5 MINS
COOK TIME : 0 MINS

4 pickled guindilla peppers
12 anchovies in oil, drained
24 pitted manzanilla or nocellara olives
Extra-virgin olive oil, for drizzling
Orange zest, for sprinkling

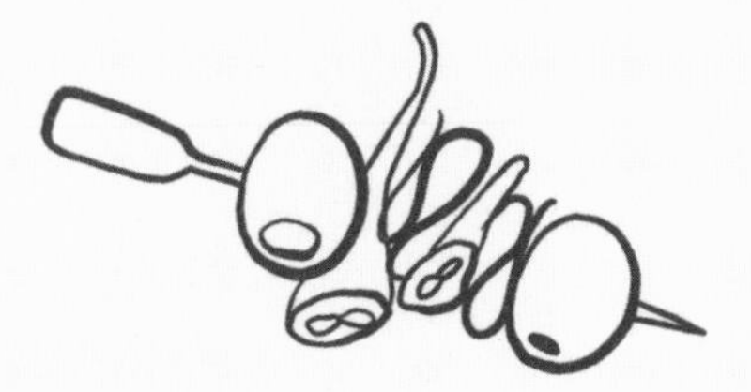

Effortlessly fancy and chic, this little Basque pinxto is more than the sum of its parts. Spend a few minutes before your guests arrive threading these onto small toothpicks or better still, use some reusable mini skewers before serving.

Cut the guindilla peppers into 6 pieces and the anchovies in half. Skewer an olive, then an anchovy half, then 2 guindilla pieces, the remaining anchovy half, then another olive and repeat.

Drizzle with extra-virgin olive oil if serving immediately, otherwise, store submerged in olive oil, then remove and drain some of the oil off before serving on a small serving plate, sprinkled with a little orange zest.

MAKE AHEAD:
You can make these the day before, but be sure to submerge them in olive oil and cover so the anchovies don't dry out.

HEMINGWAY DAIQUIRI

MAKES : 8
PREP TIME : 5 MINS

16 ounces (475ml) white rum
4 ounces (120ml) maraschino liqueur
6 ounces (175ml) lime juice
4 ounces (120ml) grapefruit juice
Strip of grapefruit or lime wheel, for serving

The perfect cocktail to batch prepare, it was invented by a Cuban mixologist for Ernest Hemingway. Measure out the ingredients and store in the refrigerator in a pitcher. If you want to make things professional, shake in a cocktail shaker with ice cubes and pour to serve. I like to serve these in small-stemmed glasses.

Mix all the ingredients together and store in the refrigerator.

When ready to serve, either pour into small glasses or shake in a cocktail shaker with ice and pour into a small glass. Garnish with a strip of grapefruit or a wheel of lime.

MAKE AHEAD
Make 1 to 2 days ahead and store in the refrigerator until ready to use.

WHIPPED COD ROE WITH PITA CHIPS & RADISHES

SERVES : 4
PREP TIME : 10 MINS
COOK TIME : 5 MINS

3 pitas
Scant 1 cup (200ml) olive oil (mild flavor), plus extra for brushing
Paprika, for dusting
2 slices crustless white bread
5½ ounces (150g) smoked cod roe
Juice of 1 lemon
Extra-virgin olive oil, for drizzling
A bunch of radishes, for serving

There are 2 options here: you can either buy this dip ready-made in the grocery store, which is perfectly good, or if you have a little extra time and energy, then this homemade dip is very quick to whizz up. Serve with a plate of fresh radishes and some crispy homemade pita chips.

Preheat the oven to 400°F (200°C). Cut the pitas into rough strips, brush with a little olive oil, and sprinkle with a light dusting of paprika. Bake in the oven for 4 to 5 minutes until crisp.

Meanwhile, soak the bread in 2 tablespoons water until soft. Peel the membrane off the cod roe, then add the roe to a food processor with the soaked bread, squeezed dry, the lemon juice, and half the olive oil. Blitz together until very smooth, adding more olive oil as you go until it is velvety and light.

Transfer the dip to a serving bowl, drizzle with extra-virgin olive oil, and serve with the radishes and crispy pita chips.

VIRGIN CUCUMBER & MINT MOJITO

SERVES : 4
PREP TIME : 5 MINS

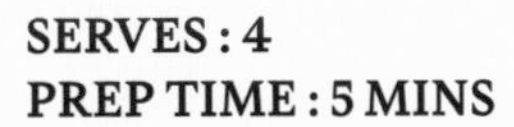

1 handful of mint leaves (save a few for garnishing)
Juice of 2 limes about ¼ cup (60ml) lime juice
10 ounces (280g) cucumber, coarsely chopped
3 tablespoons superfine sugar
Soda water

Cool as cucumber, this vibrant green mojito is summer in a glass. Serve with plenty of ice and a sprig of fresh mint—the perfect refreshing highball mocktail for a hot day.

Blitz the mint leaves, lime juice, cucumber, and sugar together in a blender. Pour in 1½ cups (350ml) water and whizz until smooth, then pass through a strainer.

Store in a pitcher in the refrigerator, or divide between highball glasses with lots of ice and top off with soda water. Add a couple of mint leaves to garnish and serve.

SLIVERED MELON & PROSCIUTTO

SERVES : 4
PREP TIME : 5 MINS
COOK TIME : 0 MINS

1 ripe cantaloupe melon
Extra-virgin olive oil, for drizzling
½ teaspoon Aleppo pepper
3 tablespoons slivered almonds
3½ ounces (100g) wafer-thin sliced prosciutto (Parma ham)

A high summer treat, ripe sweet melon meets with wafer-thin salty ham to make the perfect canapé. If you can buy your ham from the deli counter, it is the best way of ensuring that they slice it very thinly (crucial in my opinion), not only making it go further but also making sure it melts in your mouth.

Halve the melon, scoop out the seeds, then slice into ½-inch (1-cm) pieces. Using a knife, slice away the skin to be left with a half-moon piece of melon. Drizzle the melon with the olive oil, sprinkle with a few pinches of the Aleppo pepper and then the almonds. Wrap the ham around the melon slices, securing with a toothpick, if needed, then serve at once.

GET-AHEAD FROZEN MARGARITAS

SERVES : 4
PREP TIME : 5 MINS

2 limes
8 ounces (250ml) blanco tequila
4 ounces (120ml) triple sec
2 ounces (60ml) agave syrup

FOR THE GARNISH:
Salt and/or a little chile powder
1 lime, cut into wedges

These citrus cubes are an idea I've unashamedly pinched from the no-waste guru Max La Manna, though I think he had more wholesome intentions for their use—dropped into water as a soda. Naturally my mind strayed to frozen margaritas. You will need to start these the day before you serve them.

Scrub the outside of the limes, then dunk into a bowl of boiling water for 1 to 2 minutes. Cut in half, remove the seeds, then coarsely chop. Add the limes to a high-speed blender with 1 cup (250ml) water and blitz until completely smooth. Pour the juice into an ice-cube tray and freeze for at least 4 to 5 hours until solid.

For the garnish, sprinkle a few teaspoons of salt and/or chile powder over a small plate. Rub a lime wedge along the rim of your chosen glasses, then dip each glass into the salt so that the entire rim of the glass is covered. Set aside.

When ready to serve, add a handful of ice cubes to a blender with the tequila, triple sec, and agave and blend until slushy. Pour into the prepared glasses and serve, garnished with a lime wedge.

3 WAYS WITH BRUSCHETTA

Bruschetta is just an elegant way of considering things on toast, and I am a firm proponent of things that sit comfortably on toast while drinking a glass of wine or a cocktail. Admittedly, you might have to hand out a napkin with these, because the oil can be rather messy.

EACH MAKE : 12
PREP TIME : 5 MINS
COOK TIME : 5 MINS

12 slices sourdough, baguette or ciabatta
Olive oil, for brushing

Depending on the size of your bread, cut into manageable-sized pieces. You might want to leave the ciabatta slices whole. Brush the bread with olive oil. Heat a stovetop grill pan over high heat and, once hot, add the slices of bread (in batches if necessary). Press the bread into the grill pan to create dark lines and cook for 1 minute, or until charred. Flip over and repeat. Top with the toppings below and serve.

GRATED TOMATO "PAN CON TOMATE"

2 large beefsteak tomatoes
1 garlic clove, sliced in half
Extra-virgin olive oil, for drizzling
Flaky sea salt

Using a box grater, grate the tomatoes into a large bowl, leaving behind the outer skin. Season with salt.

Rub the garlic halves all over one side of the toasted bread. Spoon the grated tomatoes over the toasts, drizzle with extra-virgin olive oil, and serve.

STRACCIATELLA, ANCHOVY & FRIED SAGE

7-ounce (220-g) tub stracciatella cheese or 1 large ball mozzarella
12 anchovies in oil, drained
1 tablespoon olive oil
12 sage leaves

Spread the stracciatella in a layer over the toasted bread, then add an anchovy to each.

Heat the olive oil in a skillet over medium heat, add the sage leaves, and fry for 1 minute, or until crisp. Add to the top of each toast and serve.

ARTICHOKE, LEMON & RICOTTA

24 artichoke pieces in oil (from a 10-ounce/280-g jar)
1 tablespoon olive oil
4 tablespoons ricotta
1 handful of arugula
Juice of ½ lemon
2 tablespoons shaved Parmesan
Salt and black pepper

Drain the artichokes and pat dry with paper towels. Heat the olive oil in a skillet over medium heat, add the artichokes, and fry for 2 minutes on each side until golden. Spread a thin layer of ricotta over each toast, then add 2 artichokes to each and a few arugula leaves. Drizzle with lemon juice and plenty of salt and pepper. Finish with a few shards of Parmesan.

GRAPEFRUIT PORTO TONICO

SERVES : 1
PREP TIME : 5 MINS

1½ ounces (45ml) dry white port
2 wedges pink grapefruit
3 ounces (90ml) tonic water or club soda

Fill a low glass with ice, add the port, then squeeze the juice from 1 grapefruit wedge. Top off with the tonic water. Serve with the other wedge of grapefruit tucked into the glass.

FIGS WITH GORGONZOLA & SALTED MAPLE PECANS

SERVES : 4
PREP TIME : 5 MINS
COOK TIME : 10 MINS

½ cup (65g) pecans
2 tablespoons maple syrup
½ teaspoon chopped rosemary
12 ripe (best you can get) figs
6 tablespoons gorgonzola
Flaky sea salt

I like to use gorgonzola "cucchaio," named as such for its creaminess to the point of a spoon being the only suitable implement to distribute it! However, if you can't find it, a normal creamy gorgonzola will do the trick here.

Preheat the oven to 375°F (190°C).

Spread the pecans out on a baking sheet and toast in the oven for 6 to 8 minutes until toasted and slightly darker. Add the maple syrup, chopped rosemary, and salt to taste, then toss the hot nuts in the mixture. Return to the oven for 1 to 2 minutes until sticky and browned. Decant the nuts onto a cutting board and coarsely chop.

Tear the figs in half, or if you want to be neat, cut them into slices. Add a spoonful of gorgonzola to each fig, then top with the chopped nut crumb. Serve at once.

SAGE & CITRUS SPRITZ

SERVES : 4
PREP TIME : 5 MINS

1 pink grapefruit
28 to 32 sage leaves
2 teaspoons demerara or turbinado sugar
Soda water

There's something very soothing about the scent of fresh sage, and by muddling it with the sugar for this spritzy soda, it releases all those gentle aromas. This drink is best served in a highball glass with plenty of ice.

Halve the grapefruit and squeeze the juice from one half. Slice the remaining half into thick circles, then cut the circles into triangles.

In each highball glass, add 7 to 8 sage leaves and ½ teaspoon of the sugar. Using a muddler or the base of a rolling pin, crush the sage leaves into the sugar. Add 3 grapefruit triangles to each glass and crush them too. Add a quarter of the grapefruit juice and a few ice cubes, then top off with soda water. Stir to combine. Serve.

3-INGREDIENT WHIPPED FETA DIP

SERVES : 4
PREP TIME : 5 MINS
COOK TIME : 0 MINS

3½ ounces (100g) feta, crumbled
6 tablespoons thick Greek yogurt
Zest of ½ lemon
1 teaspoon lemon juice
Crudités, potato chips, pita chips, or flatbreads, for serving

FOR A VARIATION:
1 to 2 tablespoons Dukkah (page 193)
Extra-virgin olive oil
8 torn pitted green olives
a few toasted coriander seeds
2 tablespoons toasted sesame seeds
Coarsely cracked black pepper

This fuss-free dip packs a big punch and pairs well with really crisp and crunchy crudités, particularly celery, fennel, radishes, and cucumber. You can add the raw accompaniments to a bowl of ice water for 15 minutes before serving, which crisps them up. The whipped feta is excellent as it is, or try topping it with a few little ideas (see left) to jazz it up. s

Whizz the feta in a food processor until fairly smooth. Add the yogurt, whizz again until velvety smooth, then stir through the lemon zest and juice. Transfer to a bowl and chill until ready to serve. Remove from the refrigerator for a few minutes before serving, as it firms up in the refrigerator.

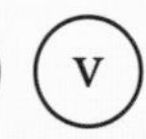

FIERY GINGER & LEMONGRASS ICED TEA

SERVES : 4
PREP TIME : 5 MINS

4 lemongrass stalks
4-inch (10-cm) piece of gingerroot, peeled and coarsely chopped
Juice of 1 lemon
3 to 4 teaspoons honey
Lemon wedges, for serving

This tastes like goodness distilled, which is also to say, that it's not for the fainthearted and certainly wards off any incoming colds. I like to serve this tea chilled over ice, but it is also good warm on a cold fall day.

Remove the tough outer leaves and base of the lemongrass stalks and chop into 1-inch (2.5-cm) long pieces. Add to a blender with the ginger, lemon juice, and honey. Add 3 cups (750ml) water and blend. Strain into a pitcher and store in the refrigerator. Serve over ice with a lemon wedge.

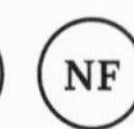

CHILE JAM & BLUE CHEESE TWISTS

MAKES : 20
PREP TIME : 5 MINS
COOK TIME : 15 MINS

- 1 sheet puff pastry, 12 ounces/350g (brands vary—look for all butter)
- 4 tablespoons chile jam
- 3½ ounces (100g) blue cheese
- 1 egg, beaten

To make these crunchy cheesy canapés extra elegant, use an all-butter puff pastry and some good-quality blue cheese.

Preheat the oven to 350°F (180°C).

Line 2 sheet pans with baking parchment. Roll the puff pastry out, spoon the chile jam onto the pastry, and spread it thinly over the entire surface. Sprinkle the blue cheese over the top, pressing it in very lightly to help it stick when you twist.

Using a pizza cutter or a knife, slice the pastry into ¾-inch (2-cm) strips. Take each strip and twist it into a spiral. Lay it on the lined sheet pans, leaving 1 to 2 inches (2.5 to 5cm) between them. Brush the exposed outside of the pastry with beaten egg, then bake in the oven for 15 minutes, or until golden and crisp, switching the pans around halfway so that they crisp evenly. Let cool slightly before serving warm.

HIBISCUS COOLER

SERVES : 4
PREP TIME : 5 MINS
COOK TIME : 5 MINS

- 2 handfuls (20g) of dried hibiscus flowers
- ½ cup (100g) granulated sugar
- Juice of 3 limes
- Water or club soda, for diluting

Nothing says "summertime gathering" more than a tumbler of one of these perky pink and limey cocktails. Serve in a large pitcher filled with lots of ice.

Put the hibiscus flowers in a saucepan with a generous 2 cups (500ml) water and the sugar. Bring to a very low simmer for 5 minutes. Set aside to let the flowers steep and cool. Once cool, add the lime juice. When ready to serve, pour into a big pitcher over lots of ice. Top off with a little water or club soda.

THE BIG SHARING ANTIPASTO PLATTER

This Italian antipasto platter mostly relies on access to a good-quality Italian deli counter and some artful skewering, swirling, and spreading. To make this go further as a sharing main course, add the bruschetta on page 26, the slivered melon on page 24, or the figs on page 31.

THE BIG SHARING ANTIPASTO PLATTER

SERVES : 4
PREP TIME : 15 MINS
COOK TIME : 0 MINS

12 cherry tomatoes
4 basil sprigs
12 bocconcini (little mozzarella balls)
Extra-virgin olive oil, for drizzling
12 slices prosciutto di Parma or San Daniele
12 grissini/breadsticks
12-ounce (350-g) jar favorite olives
1 orange
½ teaspoon coriander seeds
½ teaspoon thyme leaves
1 large piece of Parmesan
1 handful of arugula leaves
1 lemon
12 slices bresaola
7-ounce (200-g) jar black olive paste/tapenade
12 crostini/thin circles of toasted ciabatta bread
12-ounce (350-g) jar sundried tomatoes
12 boquerones anchovies
A few thyme sprigs (optional)
Salt and black pepper

FOR THE TOMATO-MOZZARELLA SKEWERS (MAKES 12):
Cut the cherry tomatoes in half and remove the leaves from the basil stems. Thread a piece of tomato, followed by a torn basil leaf, a ball of mozzarella, and a basil leaf onto a toothpick or small bamboo skewer, then finish with another tomato piece. Drizzle with olive oil and finish with cracked black pepper.

PROSCIUTTO GRISSINI STICKS (MAKES 12):
Take a piece of prosciutto and wrap it all the way around a grissini leaving just enough space at the bottom to hold it. (Don't do this too far ahead of time or the ham will dry out. If making these more than 30 minutes before serving, be sure to cover in plastic wrap.)

SPRUCE UP YOUR OLIVES:
Drain the olives and add to a small dish. Use a vegetable peeler to remove 2 strips of zest from an orange and slice into thin ribbons. Toast the coriander seeds in a dry skillet for 1 minute, or until fragrant, crush lightly, and sprinkle over the olives. Add the thyme leaves and extra-virgin olive oil to make them extra glossy.

ROTOLI DI BRESAOLA (MAKES 12):
Use a vegetable peeler to make ribbony flakes of the Parmesan, then set aside. Dress the arugula leaves with a squeeze of lemon, a drizzle of extra-virgin olive oil, and seasoning. Lay a piece of bresaola on a counter and sprinkle with the Parmesan and a few of the arugula leaves. Roll up tightly and either secure with a toothpick or arrange, seam-side down, on the plate or platter.

CROSTINI (MAKES 12):
Spread 1 teaspoon of olive paste on the base of each piece of crostini. Add a sundried tomato and an anchovy, and, if you have a few thyme leaves, sprinkle these over too.

MAKE AHEAD:
All of these items can be made a day ahead, except for the prosciutto grissini and the bresaola wraps. Be sure to cover them all well, especially the cured meats, as they may dry out.

TO ASSEMBLE YOUR BOARD:
I like to use a huge board or a big platter, then start by arranging all the larger items in the center, such as the bowl of olives, then add the grissini, the bresaola rolls, crostini, and finally, the skewers.

MEDITERRANEAN MEZZE PLATTER

SERVES 4 FOR DINNER, OR 8 AS AN APPETIZER
PREP TIME : 15 MINS
COOK TIME : 5 MINS

2 x 7-ounce (200-g) blocks Greek feta
Extra-virgin olive oil, for cooking and drizzling
1 red chile (fresh or dried), sliced
Zest of 1 lemon
½ teaspoon black peppercorns
9-ounce (250-g) package lavash flatbreads or pitas
Za'atar, for sprinkling (optional)
A few oregano or marjoram sprigs (optional)
17-ounce (480-g) tub your favorite hummus
17-ounce (480-g) tub tzatziki
17-ounce (480-g) tub other hummus (try beet or red bell pepper)
6-ounce (175-g) tub labneh, or strained Greek yogurt
12-ounce (350-g) jar mixed olives
12-ounce (350-g) jar artichokes in olive oil
12-ounce (350-g) jar semidried tomatoes
16 falafels, warmed
A selection of crunchy vegetables

IDEAS FOR TOPPING YOUR DIPS:

- Extra-virgin olive oil
- Dukkah (good piled onto labneh with extra-virgin olive oil)
- Za'atar
- Toasted sesame seeds
- Sweet smoked paprika
- Caramelized red onion jam
- Roasted or raw garbanzo beans (roast in olive, salt, and pepper until crunchy)
- Crushed toasted nuts

MARINATE YOUR FETA:

Cut the feta into ½-inch (1-cm) cubes and put into a bowl. Heat 4 tablespoons of olive oil, sliced red chile, 4 strips of lemon zest, and the peppercorns in a small pan over low heat for 1 minute, or until warm. Spoon over the feta and stir together. Serve at once or store covered in a little extra oil and eat within 2 to 3 days.

UPGRADING YOUR FLATBREAD:

An easy way to upgrade your flatbread is a quick char on a stovetop grill pan to heat. Brush with a little olive oil and press it into the hot pan. Dust with za'atar or sprinkle with herbs to serve.

TO ASSEMBLE YOUR BOARD:

Arrange the dips and labneh in bowls as described below, then surround with your chosen crunchy vegetables. Add the flatbread, cut into shards, then serve with the marinated feta in a bowl, the olives, artichokes, sundried tomatoes, and warmed falafels.

A NOTE ON PRESENTATION

As tempting as it can be to speed things up and serve straight from the tubs, use your best crockery for this Mediterranean spread. I like to decant the dips into shallow bowls or plates: Dollop a few spoonfuls of the dip into the center of the plate or bowl and, using the back of a spoon, swirl the plate around to spread the dip out across the plate, leaving a higher edge at the sides. This creates a crater for you to drizzle extra-virgin olive oil, spices, or other condiments into, and then it is easy to scoop it with some flatbread or crunchy raw vegetables.

MEDITERRANEAN MEZZE PLATTER

With the range of good-quality dips, falafel, olives, and other snacks in grocery stores these days, one of my go-to entertaining hacks when time is limited is to embellish a few store-bought purchases with a few food-styling tricks to make a low-effort spread look indulgent.

BAKED CAMEMBERT BOARD WITH DIPS

One of the most relaxed and sociable ways to entertain is by artfully arranging a spread of food onto a large platter or board and leaving people to help themselves. Pair this with a pitcher of cocktails and it's the help-yourself dinner to delight both hosts and guests alike.

BAKED CAMEMBERT BOARD WITH DIPS

SERVES : 4 FOR DINNER, OR 8 AS AN APPETIZER
PREP TIME : 15 MINS
COOK TIME : 30 MINS

2 x 8-ounces (225-g) good-quality Camembert cheese wheels
A splash of dry white wine/ vermouth
4 bushy thyme sprigs
4 tablespoons chopped walnuts

FOR THE CHEESE:
Preheat the oven to 375°F (190°C). Remove the Camembert from their packaging and add a few slits to the top of them. Place in an ovenproof dish, add a splash of wine, a few thyme sprigs, and the walnuts. Place on a sheet pan and bake for 20 minutes, or until very soft (although this will depend slightly on the ripeness of your cheese, so give it a little press, it should feel very squidgy).

Serve with all the accompaniments below.

- 1 cucumber
- 5 celery stalks
- 2 baby gem lettuce or mini romaine
- 1 lemon
- 1 ciabatta loaf
- 1 bunch radishes
- 1 small head fennel
- 2 sweet bell peppers
- 1 bunch of baby carrots
- 1 cup (100g) frozen cranberries
- 2 handfuls of small baby new potatoes
- 1 tablespoon butter
- Some cold cuts

LEMONY CRUNCHY CUCUMBER & CELERY SALAD:
Use a vegetable peeler to peel away strips of the cucumber skin to create a stripy effect. Slice in half lengthwise, then scoop out the seeds from the cucumber. Slice into ¼-inch (5-mm) pieces. Slice the celery into similar-size pieces at an angle. Separate the leaves from the lettuce and put into a salad bowl with the celery and cucumber. Toss well with the juice of 1 lemon and a few drizzles of olive oil. Season with salt and pepper and serve.

GRILLED TOASTS:
For extra fancy toast look no further than a hot stovetop grill pan for the dramatic char lines. Slice the ciabatta at an angle into ¼-inch (5-mm) slices. Heat a stovetop grill pan until smoky hot, drizzle a batch of the ciabatta with oil, and lay across the hot grill pan. Use the back of a spatula to press the pieces down on the pan, then flip them over and repeat on the other side until you have lovely char lines over the bread.

CRUDITÉS:
The crunchier and fresher the better when it comes to crudités. I'm opting for some radishes, fennel, red bell peppers, and carrot here. Peel and store in a bowl of ice water in the refrigerator. They will be extra crisp and crunchy. Just drain them and serve alongside the cheese in a bowl with a clean cloth to catch the excess water. They will stay super fresh.

QUICK CRANBERRY JAM:
Put the frozen cranberries into a small saucepan, add 3 tablespoons sugar, cover with a lid, and cook over low heat for 5 to 10 minutes until the cranberries soften and burst into a tart-sweet jam. Let cool, then serve with the cheese.

POTATOES:
Put the potatoes into a saucepan of cold salted water. Bring to a boil, then reduce the heat and simmer for 10 to 12 minutes until tender to the point of a sharp knife. Drain and dress with the butter and plenty of salt and pepper.

MAKE AHEAD:
Make the potatoes and cranberry jam up to 2 days ahead. Leave yourself 15 minutes to prepare the final bits, salad, crudités, and put the Camembert into the oven.

ASSEMBLE:
With the cheeses as the centerpiece, I like to serve them with the colorful crudités, grilled toasts, and cranberry jam gathered around the outside. Arrange the cold cuts on the same serving platter, then the salad and potatoes in bowls on the side.

Any grapes, figs, crunchy pickles, dried fruits, or nuts are also an excellent addition to the board.

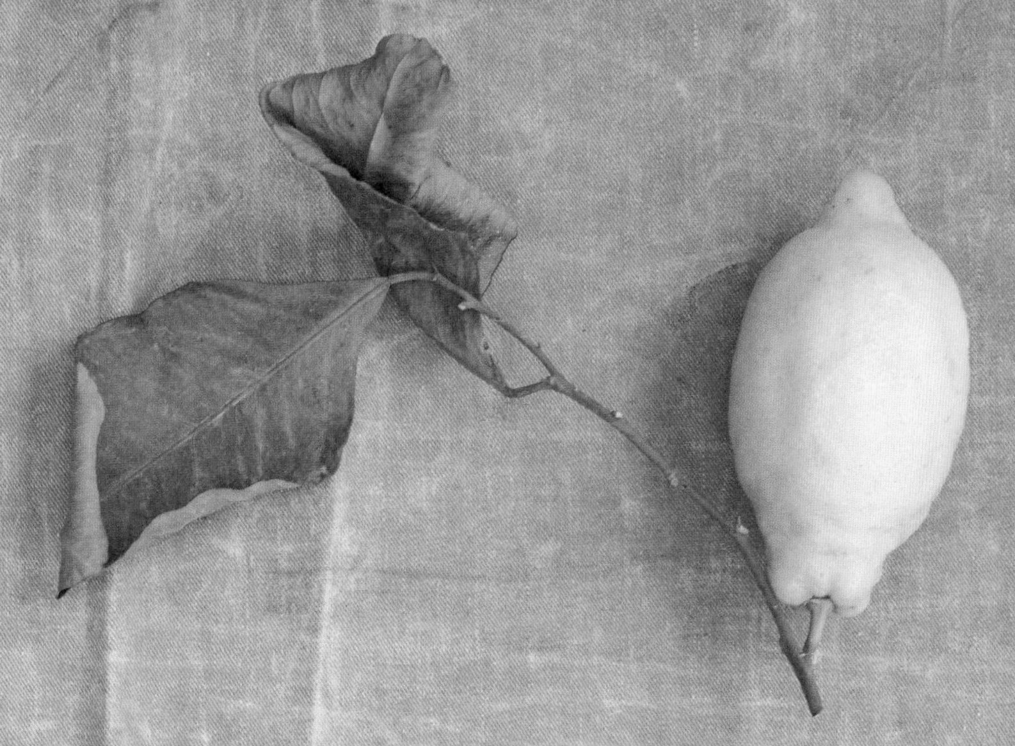

APPETIZERS

ASPARAGUS WITH CREAMY ALMOND TARATOR

Almond tarator is one of the all-time great pantry sauces. Here, it is used as a nutty, creamy base to some beautifully green asparagus. I like to toast a few extra slivered almonds to sprinkle over the top of the finished dish, but the Dukkah on page 193 would also work well.

SERVES : 4
PREP TIME : 12 MINS
COOK TIME : 5 MINS

1 slice white bread, crust removed
1 cup (90g) blanched almonds, toasted
1 garlic clove, peeled
3 to 4 tablespoons lemon juice
¾ cup (175ml) extra-virgin olive oil
2 bunches of asparagus
Salt
2 tablespoons toasted slivered almonds, for serving

For the sauce, soak the bread in a little water and squeeze dry. Add the soaked bread to a blender with the almonds, garlic, lemon juice, and olive oil and whizz. If it's too thick, thin with a little water. Add salt to taste.

Trim or break off the woody ends of the asparagus, then blanch them in a pan of salted water until they turn a vibrant green and still have a little bite. When they are done, drain and plunge them into a bowl of ice water as this will keep them exceptionally green.

Spoon the sauce onto a serving platter or individual plates, then divide the asparagus spears either among the plates or pile them onto the platter and serve, sprinkled with toasted almonds.

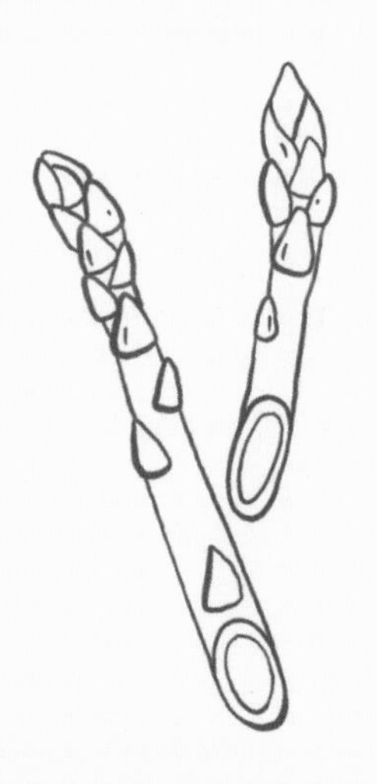

MAKE AHEAD:
The tarator can be made 2 to 3 days ahead and stored in the refrigerator. It may harden up so leave at room temperature for 15 minutes before serving.

SUBS:
You can use walnuts or hazelnuts instead of almonds, if desired, but none are quite as creamy as almonds.

PHYLLO-FRIED FETA WITH A TOMATO-CAPER SALAD

Once you have tried this technique of wrapping feta in phyllo pastry, you will be going back to it time and time again. The feta softens in the crispy outer shell of the pastry, and the salty-sweet combination with the honey is very moreish. I use citrusy sumac here, but you can spice it up with a few hot pepper flakes or sesame seeds, if you prefer.

SERVES : 2
PREP TIME : 15 MINS
COOK TIME : 5 MINS

2 large beefsteak tomatoes, sliced
3 tablespoons caperberries
1 shallot, thinly sliced
1 tablespoon extra-virgin olive oil, plus extra for serving
7-ounce (200-g) block of feta
1 sheet of phyllo pastry
2 tablespoons olive oil
½ teaspoon sumac
1 tablespoon honey
4 oregano or thyme sprigs
Salt and black pepper

Add the tomatoes, caperberries, and shallot to a large bowl. Toss with a couple of pinches of salt and the extra-virgin olive oil, then season with pepper. Set aside.

Pat the feta dry with paper towels—you need it fairly dry or the pastry won't crisp. Lay a sheet of phyllo out on a counter and brush with 1 tablespoon of the olive oil. Lay the feta in the center, sprinkle with sumac, and wrap it up like you are wrapping a birthday present. Brush the edges so it's well sealed and trim away to about ¾ inches (2cm) off either short side.

Heat a nonstick skillet with the remaining tablespoon of olive oil over low heat. Once the oil is hot, add the phyllo-wrapped feta, and cook for 2 minutes, or until lightly golden on all sides. Add the honey and oregano or thyme and spoon over the feta for 30 seconds, or until it is coated and sticky. Transfer to a board.

Serve half of the feta per person with the tomato and caper salad and a little more extra-virgin olive oil.

CRISPY GYOZA SALAD WITH A ZIPPY THAI-STYLE DRESSING

Little packages of gyoza are a freezer favorite of mine. Quick to cook and easy to adapt to different dining occasions like this hot and zesty appetizer or the winter warmer in a broth on page 93. If you have some fresh salad leaves and a handful of herbs these would be an excellent addition, but here I have stuck to the longer-life vegetable bits you might have in your refrigerator drawer.

SERVES : 4
PREP TIME : 12 MINS
COOK TIME : 5 MINS

¼ red or white cabbage
2 carrots
1 large or 2 small beets
20 vegetable gyoza
1 tablespoon sesame seeds, toasted

THAI-STYLE DRESSING:

1 tablespoon superfine sugar
1 tablespoon fish sauce
1 red chile, finely chopped
Juice of 2 to 3 limes

For the dressing, whisk the sugar, fish sauce, chile, and lime juice together in a bowl or shake in a jar.

Use a mandoline or very finely slice the cabbage, carrots, and beets and mix together in a large bowl. Add the dressing and toss until the salad is well coated. Set aside.

Cook the gyoza according to the package directions. I opt for the crisping in the pan option. Fry the gyoza for 1 to 2 minutes, then add a small amount of water, cover with a lid, and steam until all the liquid has evaporated.

Serve the gyoza next to the salad, then sprinkle the sesame seeds over the top.

MAKE AHEAD:

Finely slice the vegetables up to 8 hours before and store under a damp cloth or paper towels in the refrigerator. You can also make the dressing and store it in a jar in the refrigerator for up to a day in advance.

BURRATA WITH BEET & GRATED TOMATO

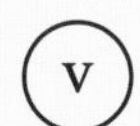

Grating tomatoes for simple salsas or sauces is a great timesaver. Season the tomatoes with a little salt, then sprinkle over the beets and you have an elegant appetizer all ready in under 10 minutes. This is perfect served with some fresh crusty bread.

SERVES : 4
PREP TIME : 10 MINS
COOK TIME : 0 MINS

2 large ripe tomatoes
4 small cooked beets (vacuum packed)
2 teaspoons sherry vinegar
4 small burrata balls (or 2 large halved)
2 tablespoons Dukkah (page 193)
Extra-virgin olive oil, for drizzling
Salt and black pepper

Using a box grater, grate the tomato into a bowl and season with a pinch of salt. Set aside while you prepare the rest of the dish.

Chop the beets into wedges, add to a bowl, and toss in the sherry vinegar and a pinch each of salt and pepper. Set aside.

To assemble, place a ball of burrata on each plate. Add the beets to one side, then dress with the tomato. Sprinkle with the dukkah, black pepper, and drizzle with extra-virgin olive oil.

SUBS:
Don't have any dukkah? Toasted sesame seeds work a treat here—simply toast some sesame seeds in a dry skillet for a few minutes.

WATERMELON, SALTED RICOTTA & MINT SALAD

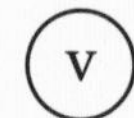

This is an ideal high summer assembly salad, when it's far too hot to cook. A firm, salted ricotta works brilliantly with the sweet, tender flesh of the watermelon, but if you can't find ricotta a more conventional feta will also do the trick. Be sure to store your watermelon in the refrigerator so it is very cold before serving.

SERVES : 4
PREP TIME : 15 MINS
COOK TIME : 0 MINS

2 shallots, peeled
1 tablespoon red wine vinegar
Pinch of superfine sugar
1 mini to small watermelon, about 2 pounds (900g)
3½ ounces (100g) salted ricotta or feta
8 mint sprigs, leaves picked
Extra-virgin olive oil, for drizzling
Salt and black pepper

Slice the shallots very finely into circles, about ¼ inch (5mm) thick, and place in a small bowl. Drizzle with the vinegar and a pinch of salt and sugar. Set aside while you prepare the rest of the salad.

Slice the watermelon in half, then slice the skin away from the flesh and discard. Slice into pieces about ¼ inch (5mm) thick, then arrange on a serving plate or divide among individual plates. Shave the ricotta finely over the top and sprinkle with the mint leaves. Add the pickled shallots, then drizzle with plenty of extra-virgin olive oil and lots of coarsely cracked black pepper. Serve.

MAKE AHEAD:
I like to prepare the watermelon slices a few hours ahead and leave, covered, in the refrigerator to chill until ready to serve. You can also make the pickled shallots a few hours ahead, if desired.

SUBS:
Swap the shallots for a small red onion and prepare in the same way as the shallots.

SMASHED CUCUMBER, SESAME & CILANTRO SALAD

VG  

If you haven't smashed a cucumber before, you've not lived. This technique allows the salt to penetrate the cucumber's flesh, drawing out the water, all the while seasoning it at the same time. The firmer and sweeter the cucumber the better for this refreshing salad. This salad is also great served alongside the Caramel-glazed duck legs (page 132) and the Broiled chicken skewers (page 75).

SERVES : 4
PREP TIME : 25 MINS
COOK TIME : 2 MINS

1 cucumber (1 pound/450g), Persian or Lebanese work best
½ teaspoon sea salt
1 garlic clove, finely chopped
1 tablespoon light soy sauce
1 tablespoon rice vinegar
1 tablespoon toasted sesame oil
2 tablespoons sesame seeds
1 handful of cilantro leaves
2 tablespoons Homemade chili sauce (page 196), for serving (optional)

Trim the cucumbers then place on a cutting board. Using a rolling pin, bash the cucumber until it breaks apart, then tear the cucumber into bite-size pieces, or chop them if they don't come apart very easily. Add the cucumber to a colander, toss with the salt, and let stand for 10 minutes.

Meanwhile, put the garlic, soy sauce, vinegar, and sesame oil into a large bowl. Shake the excess water off the cucumber in the colander and add to the bowl.

Toast the sesame seeds in a small skillet over low heat for 2 minutes, or until golden. Add to the bowl, then add the cilantro leaves and serve with chili sauce, if desired.

SPANISH TOMATO SOUP WITH SERRANO HAM CRISP

This refreshing summer soup is a great one to make in advance. The flavor of the garlic intensifies the longer it lingers in the soup, so think about using slightly less if making the soup more than 12 hours in advance. While this soup is perfectly delicious on its own, the little Serrano ham crisp gives it more of a "dinner party" fanfare.

SERVES : 4
PREP TIME : 10 MINS
COOK TIME : 18 MINS

4 slices Serrano or prosciutto
2 eggs (optional)
1½ pounds (675g) ripe tomatoes, coarsely chopped
1 to 2 garlic cloves, peeled
½ teaspoon salt
3 tablespoons extra-virgin olive oil
A splash of sherry vinegar, to taste

Preheat the oven to 375°F (190°C). Line a baking sheet with baking parchment. Lay the slices of ham out over the lined sheet and cook in the oven for 10 to 12 minutes until crisp. Cook the eggs now for 8 minutes, if using, and peel. Chop into small pieces. Set aside.

Blitz the tomatoes, garlic (see introduction above), salt, and olive oil in a blender until very smooth. Add the vinegar to taste.

Divide the soup among shallow bowls. Sprinkle with the chopped egg and the crispy ham, broken into shards, and serve.

MAKE AHEAD:
Make this up to 2 days in advance and store in the refrigerator. You can also boil the eggs ahead, but the ham crisp is best served fresh.

WHITE ASPARAGUS VICHYSSOISE

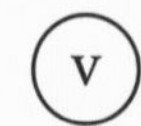

This classically French soup has survived the test of time for very good reason. Creamy and unctuous, it's more than the sum of its modest parts. Comforting when served hot, and refreshing when cold, my spin on it swaps the leek for asparagus, giving it some more decadence for a dinner party. I've made the cream optional here to suit the mood, and if you don't whizz it into the soup, then drizzle it over as a garnish. Whizz this soup as long as time permits to make it silky smooth.

SERVES : 4
PREP TIME : 10 MINS
COOK TIME : 20 MINS

½ stick (60g) butter
1 onion, sliced
4 thick white asparagus spears, or 8 green asparagus spears
2 medium potatoes, peeled
3 plump garlic cloves, sliced
2 cups (475ml) hot light vegetable or chicken stock
½ cup (120ml) heavy cream (optional)
Salt

FOR THE GARNISH:

A few snippings of chives
Cracked black pepper
Extra-virgin olive oil

Heat the butter in a heavy-bottomed pan over low heat. Once the butter is foaming, add the onion and a pinch of salt, and cook for 6 to 7 minutes.

Meanwhile, slice the asparagus and potatoes into thin circles. Add to the onion in the pan with the garlic and cook for another 2 minutes, turning them in the butter.

Add the stock and bring to a simmer until the vegetables are just tender. Transfer to a blender with the cream, if using, and whizz until it is very silky smooth.

Divide the soup among bowls, garnish with a few snips of chives, coarse black pepper, and a swirl of extra-virgin olive oil. Serve either hot or cold.

MAKE AHEAD:

Make up to 3 days in advance and store in the refrigerator. This also freezes well for up to 6 months. Be sure to heat it until piping hot if defrosting.

WEDGE SALAD & BLUE CHEESE DRESSING

A simple and an ever-satisfying way to start a meal; this wedge salad is crunchy, cool, and a surefire crowd-pleaser. My twist on a classic gets a lox makeover with the bagel seasoning on page 193. You can serve this with or without the smoked salmon, or you can add smoked mackerel or trout as they work a treat.

SERVES : 4
PREP TIME : 10 MINS
COOK TIME : 0 MINS

Pinch of superfine sugar
2 teaspoons red wine vinegar
½ red onion, finely sliced
1 iceberg lettuce
4 slices lox (optional)
2 tablespoons Everything bagel seasoning (page 193)

BLUE CHEESE DRESSING:
3½ ounces (100g) blue cheese
⅓ cup (75g) sour cream
2 tablespoons (30g) mayonnaise
Black pepper

Combine the sugar and 1 teaspoon of the vinegar in a bowl. Add the sliced red onion and toss to coat. Set aside.

For the dressing, crumble the blue cheese in a bowl or a food processor (if you prefer it very smooth), add the cream and mayonnaise, and stir together until smooth (there will be the odd lump, but don't worry). Add the remaining vinegar to taste and plenty of black pepper. Set aside.

Cut the lettuce into 4 wedges, removing any outer leaves. Divide among plates, cover in the dressing, and add the lox, if using. Sprinkle with the pickled red onion and bagel seasoning and serve.

MAKE AHEAD:
You can make the blue cheese dressing up to 2 days in advance and store in the refrigerator.

ON THE TABLE IN 20

SPICED PANEER & GARBANZO BEANS IN A CILANTRO BROTH

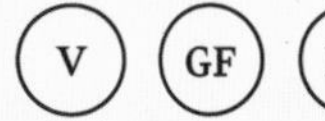

If you have already made the vibrant Lemongrass & cilantro paste (page 190) and it's stashed in the freezer, then this is perfect to pep up a couple of cans of garbanzo beans. Pair that with some frozen spinach and paneer and you have a flavorsome supper in no time at all.

SERVES : 4
PREP TIME : 5 MINS
COOK TIME : 15 MINS

7½-ounce (220-g) package paneer
1 teaspoon ground turmeric
1 teaspoon mild chile powder
Olive oil, for cooking
2 x 14-ounce (400-g) cans garbanzo beans, drained
½ cup (120g) Lemongrass & cilantro paste (page 190)
14-ounce (400-g) can coconut milk
1 handful of frozen spinach, defrosted

FOR SERVING:
Thai basil leaves
Lime wedges
Crispy shallots (page 197), (optional)
Flatbreads (optional)

Cut the paneer into 1-inch (2.5-cm) cubes, then toss in the turmeric and chile powder.

Heat a splash of olive oil in a large skillet over high heat, add the paneer, and cook for 2 to 3 minutes until golden. Add the garbanzo beans to the skillet, then take off the heat and set aside. Remove the paneer from the pan and set aside on a plate.

Add a good splash of oil to a medium high-sided saucepan, add the lemongrass paste, and cook for 3 to 4 minutes, stirring so it doesn't burn, then add the coconut milk. Refill the can halfway with water to swirl it out, then pour it into the pan. Simmer for 10 minutes, adding the spinach and garbanzo beans after 5 minutes. Finally, add the fried paneer.

Serve with a handful of basil leaves, lime wedges, crispy shallots, and flatbreads, if desired.

SUBS:
You can substitute extra-firm tofu for the paneer and prepare it in the same manner, making it a great vegan option.

BITTER LEAF SALAD WITH LIMA BEANS & ANCHOVY CRUMBS

A warming winter salad with all the right textures, this is another excellent use for my favorite "fresher-for-longer" leaf. The bitterness of the radicchio goes exceptionally well with the creamy blistered lima beans and a punch of salty crunch from the panko and anchovies.

SERVES : 4
PREP TIME : 5 MINS
COOK TIME : 8 MINS

1 large head of radicchio or chioggia
2 x 14-ounce (400-g) cans lima or butter beans, drained
Extra-virgin olive oil
4 tablespoons panko bread crumbs
8 anchovies in oil, drained and coarsely chopped
2 tablespoons Italian parsley, finely chopped
Juice of ½ lemon
Salt and black pepper

Separate the salad leaves, wash and dry, then set aside. Pat the drained beans dry with paper towels (this will help them crisp).

Add 1 tablespoon of the olive oil to a large heavy skillet and heat over high heat until the oil is very hot. Add the beans (do this in 2 batches if your pan isn't big enough—you need all the beans to have pan contact) and cook for 4 to 5 minutes, or until the beans look blistered, tossing them around the pan to evenly brown them. Transfer to a bowl, season with salt, and set aside.

Wipe the pan clean, then add another 2 tablespoons of oil. Add the panko bread crumbs and chopped anchovies and cook over medium heat for 2 minutes, or until golden. Stir in the parsley.

Arrange the salad leaves on a large serving plate or platter, drizzle with oil, then the lemon juice over the top. Sprinkle over the beans, followed by the crispy panko crumbs and serve.

SPICED BUTTER EGGS WITH LENTILS & CRISPY SHALLOTS

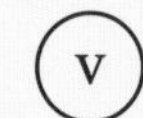

Precooked legumes are a great cheat to have to hand. You can batch cook your own and store in the freezer, or just buy from your local store. Serve these lentils with flatbreads, brushed with a little of the butter for extra indulgence, to mop up all the sauces.

SERVES : 4
PREP TIME : 5 MINS
COOK TIME : 10 MINS

1 pound (450g) cooked Puy lentils (can be bought cooked in pouches)
4 eggs
1 cup (225g) plain Greek yogurt
2 garlic cloves, 1 grated and 1 crushed
1 lime
1 stick (115g) butter
½ teaspoon ground turmeric
½ teaspoon mild chile powder
½ teaspoon cumin seeds
½ teaspoon coriander seeds
¼ teaspoon hot pepper flakes
1 handful of mixed soft herbs (page 11), coarsely chopped
3 tablespoons Crispy shallots (page 197)
Salt and black pepper
4 flatbreads, for serving

Lightly warm the cooked lentils according to the package directions. Season with salt and pepper.

Boil the eggs in a saucepan of boiling water for 6 minutes, then drain. Meanwhile, mix the yogurt, grated garlic, the juice of half of the lime, and a pinch of salt together in a bowl. Set aside.

Put the lentils onto a large serving plate and dollop the yogurt over them. Peel the eggs, halve them, and arrange on top.

In a small pan, heat the butter with the turmeric, chile powder, cumin, coriander, hot pepper flakes, and the crushed garlic clove over low heat for 2 to 3 minutes, or until the butter is foamy and the garlic is sizzling. Pour the melted butter mixture over the dish so everything gets a good drenching in the butter. Sprinkle with the coarsely chopped herbs and crispy shallots and serve with the remaining lime half and flatbreads.

TIP:

If using uncooked lentils, use 1⅓ cups (250g) uncooked lentils as the equivalent, then simmer in a large saucepan of salted water for 15 to 20 minutes until tender. Drain.

BROILED CHICKEN SKEWERS WITH CHARRED LETTUCE

These spiced chicken skewers are excellent cooked on a stovetop grill pan or griddle. You can vary the accompaniments to suit what's in the refrigerator—a spicy slaw like the one on page 52, and the smashed cucumber salad on page 58, all work beautifully. Alternatively, try charring a crisp lettuce like little gem for a smoky spin.

SERVES : 4
PREP TIME : 10 MINS
COOK TIME : 15 MINS

- 4 large boneless chicken thigh fillets, 5 ounces (140g) each thigh
- 6 tablespoons Turmeric & ginger paste (page 190)
- ½ small red cabbage
- Juice of 2 limes
- 2 little gem lettuces, halved
- Olive oil, for brushing
- Sea salt and pepper
- Rice or flatbreads, for serving

The morning you want to cook the chicken, soak 8 bamboo skewers in a bowl of cold water. Slice the chicken thighs into bite-size pieces and add to a large bowl. Add 6 tablespoons of the turmeric paste and let marinate.

Meanwhile, finely shred the red cabbage on a mandoline and toss in the lime juice and a pinch of salt. Set aside.

Thread the chicken pieces onto the soaked bamboo skewers. Heat a stovetop grill pan to high and grill the skewers on all sides, turning them every 3 to 4 minutes until cooked through and charred on the outside. Remove from the pan and set aside, then brush the baby lettuces with oil and grill them on the grill pan for 2 minutes, or until char lines appear. Serve the skewers, cabbage, and lettuce with rice or flatbreads.

MAKE AHEAD:
The skewers can be made up to 2 days in advance and stored in an airtight container in the refrigerator—the flavor will be even better.

SALMON WITH HERBY CRÈME FRAÎCHE & SALTED CUCUMBER

A perfectly cooked piece of salmon is seared on the outside and still a little pink on the inside. I like to get the salmon skin crispy, which is best achieved by taking care to pat the skin dry and ensuring that it goes into a hot nonstick pan with a good splash of oil to sizzle it.

SERVES : 4
PREP TIME : 5 MINS
COOK TIME : 10 MINS

1 cucumber
2 large handfuls of new potatoes
1½ tablespoons dill, plus a few sprigs for the cucumber
3 tablespoons crème fraîche or sour cream
1½ tablespoons capers in brine, drained
Zest of 1 lemon
4 x 8-ounce (225-g) pieces salmon, skin-on
Canola or olive oil, for cooking
Salt and black pepper
Lemon wedges, for serving

Peel and slice the cucumber. Season with salt and set over a colander in the sink for 15 minutes while you make the rest. Put the potatoes into a large saucepan of cold, salted water and bring to a boil. Boil for 10 minutes, or until the point of a knife easily slides in. Drain. Toss the cucumber with the dill sprigs and potato.

Meanwhile, mix the crème fraîche, capers, and dill together in a large bowl. Season well and add the grated lemon zest.

Season the pieces of salmon heavily on both sides. Heat a nonstick skillet over high heat, add a good splash of oil, then add the salmon, skin-side down, and fry for 5 minutes, or until the skin is very crispy (I like to press it into the pan with a spatula to ensure it's got full contact with the pan). Turn over and just sear lightly on the other side for 2 to 3 minutes, then transfer to serving plates (I like to serve it skin-side up).

Serve the salmon with the potato and cucumber and the herby crème fraîche, and a lemon wedge.

MAKE AHEAD:
You can prepare everything ahead of time, but save the salmon cooking to the last minute for the best results—crispy skin and a lovely moist center.

SWEETHEART CABBAGE WITH WILD RICE SALAD & RAITA

Sweetheart cabbage, like other cabbage, keeps extremely well in the refrigerator, making it a very useful ingredient to rustle up for an impromptu dinner party. Here, I've roasted the cabbage in the oven as it takes on an extra complexity of flavor and a caramelized sweetness. I also like to keep a few pouches of precooked rice in the pantry for when I need a speedy dinner.

SERVES : 4
PREP TIME : 2 MINS
COOK TIME : 18 MINS

1 head sweetheart cabbage
Olive oil, for brushing
Salt and black pepper
Lemon wedges, for serving

CUCUMBER RAITA:
¼ cucumber
1 cup (225g) plain Greek yogurt
1 garlic clove, grated
1 tablespoon chopped mint
2 pinches of garam masala
Juice of ½ lime

WILD RICE:
2 cups (300g) cooked wild rice
2 tablespoons hazelnuts, toasted
2 tablespoons cranberries, soaked
2 tablespoons chopped mint
Extra-virgin olive oil, for drizzling

Preheat the oven to 425°F (220°C).

Cut the cabbage into quarters or eighths if really big. Brush the quarters with olive oil and sprinkle with salt and pepper. Arrange on a sheet pan and roast in the oven for 15 to 18 minutes, turning once, until golden and caramelized.

Meanwhile, prepare the raita. Grate the cucumber coarsely, then pat dry in paper towels. Mix all the ingredients together in a large bowl. Season to taste and set aside.

For the wild rice, mix the cooked rice, hazelnuts, cranberries, and mint together in another bowl. Drizzle with the extra-virgin olive oil and season to taste. Set aside.

Serve the cabbage with spoonfuls of the wild rice salad, the cucumber raita, and a lemon wedge on the side.

SEA BASS ACQUA PAZZA WITH ANCHO CHILE

Not all dried chiles are created equal. Ancho chiles are mild in heat but they have a rich, smoky, sweet depth, making them an interesting alternative to an ordinary fresh chile. If you can, use a variety of tomatoes and olives to make this dish extra colorful.

SERVES : 4
PREP TIME : 5 MINS
COOK TIME : 13 MINS

- Extra-virgin olive oil, for cooking and rubbing
- 4 large, about 1½ pounds (675g), sea bass or bream fillets
- 4 scallions, sliced
- 2 handfuls of cherry tomatoes, halved
- 4 garlic cloves, 3 sliced, 1 halved
- 4 tablespoons white wine (or 1 to 2 frozen wine cubes, page 13)
- ½ to 1 dried ancho chile, torn into coarse pieces
- 16 pitted green olives
- 1 tablespoon capers in brine, drained
- 1 ciabatta, sliced on the diagonal
- Salt
- A few basil leaves, for garnishing

Heat a large skillet with a lid over medium heat and add a good splash of oil. Season the fish skin, then add the fish to the hot oil, skin-side down, and cook for 2 minutes, or until the skin is nice and crispy. Remove from the pan and set the fish aside, skin-side up.

Add the scallions, cherry tomatoes, and 3 of the sliced garlic cloves and cook for 3 minutes, before adding the wine. Simmer, uncovered, for 2 to 3 minutes, then add ½ cup (120ml) water, the chile (½ to 1, depending on how spicy you like it), olives, and capers, and simmer for another 2 to 3 minutes. Arrange the fish fillets on top, skin-side up, pop the lid on, and let steam for 1 to 2 minutes until the fish is cooked but not falling apart.

Meanwhile, heat the broiler to high. Broil the ciabatta until golden with a little char, then rub with olive oil and the remaining garlic clove while still hot. Serve the fish, garnished with a few basil leaves and the ciabatta on the side.

MAKE AHEAD:
This dish is best made to order. You can prepare the base of the dish 1 to 2 days ahead up to the point of adding the fish. Cook the fish before serving.

SKILLET-FRIED GNOCCHI WITH WILD MUSHROOMS

Once you have pan-fried gnocchi, you will never boil them again. With a crispy golden outside contrasting the pleasingly chewy texture, this recipe is one of the quickest meals in the book. Prepackaged gnocchi can be found in the freezer, the chiller, or even vacuum-packed in the dried pasta aisle of the grocery store.

SERVES : 4
PREP TIME : 5 MINS
COOK TIME : 14 MINS

Olive oil, for cooking
2 large shallots, sliced
1 pound (450g) wild mushrooms, sliced
3 garlic cloves, finely sliced
8 sage sprigs
Squeeze of lemon juice
1 pound (450g) good-quality fresh gnocchi
4 tablespoons butter
1 handful of grated or shaved Parmesan
Salt and black pepper

Heat a large nonstick skillet over medium heat. Add a thin layer of olive oil to the pan, then add the shallots and cook for 4 minutes, moving them around in the pan. Add a little more oil, then add the mushrooms and cook for 3 to 4 minutes until golden and soft. Add the garlic and sage and cook for another 1 minute. Add the lemon juice, then transfer the mushrooms to a plate and set aside.

Heat another good splash of olive oil in the skillet over medium to high heat. Add the gnocchi and cook, tossing frequently, for 3 to 4 minutes until golden on the outside. Once cooked, add the butter, let it sizzle, then divide the gnocchi among serving plates with the mushrooms on top. Season and top with Parmesan.

MAKE AHEAD:
This dish is done in minutes so it is best cooked to order.

PASTA & NOODLES

CHARRED BROCCOLI RABE WITH LEMONY CACIO E PEPE

Sometimes the simplest dishes done well are the most satisfying of suppers, and this *cacio e pepe* is just that. Ready in under 10 minutes, it really is one of the quickest-to-prepare Italian dishes of all time. The trickiest part of this dish is adding the cheese. If the starchy, buttery pasta water is too hot it will go stringy, so remove from the heat before stirring in the Parmesan.

SERVES : 4
PREP TIME : 10 MINS
COOK TIME : 15 MINS

1 pound (450g) spaghetti or bucatini
2 handfuls of broccoli rabe, trimmed
Olive oil, for cooking
1 stick (100g) salted butter
2 teaspoons cracked black pepper
Juice of 1 lemon
2 cups (140g) grated Parmesan
Salt

Bring a large saucepan of salted water to a boil, add the pasta, and cook according to the package directions, minus about 1 minute (until it's just al dente as it will cook a little more in the pan). When you drain the pasta set 1 cup (250ml) water aside.

Meanwhile, cut the broccoli rabe into 2-inch (5-cm) pieces on the diagonal. Heat a heavy skillet over high heat, add 1 tablespoon olive oil, then the broccoli, pressing the broccoli into the pan as it cooks, to get a good golden crust on the outside. Flip over and do the same on the other side. I use a heavy pan to press, but you can use a vegetable press or press down hard with a spatula.

Remove the broccoli rabe from the skillet and set aside. Add the butter and pepper to the skillet and heat until the butter is melted and foaming. Add the pasta, 2/3 cup (150ml) of the reserved pasta water, and the lemon juice. Get the pasta well coated in the buttery liquid, then add the broccoli rabe to the pan, and sprinkle over the Parmesan. Remove from the heat and stir well, adding more pasta water, if needed. You want it glossy but if the Parmesan cooks too much it will go stringy. Serve at once.

CREAMY TORTELLINI WITH PANCETTA, PEAS & LEEKS

Dressing up store-bought tortellini with a creamy sauce means dinner is on the table in under 10 minutes. I've used spinach and ricotta tortellini here but you can choose any you fancy. Just make sure they are the best quality you can afford as it goes without saying that the better the tortellini, the better the final results!

SERVES : 4
PREP TIME : 2 MINS
COOK TIME : 8 MINS

Olive oil, for cooking
3½ ounces (100g) pancetta, cubed
2 leeks, sliced
2 handfuls of frozen peas
14 ounces (400g) tortellini
½ cup (120ml) dry white wine
2 heaped tablespoons mascarpone
5 basil or mint sprigs, leaves picked
Salt and black pepper

Bring a large saucepan of salted water to a boil.

Meanwhile, heat a good splash of olive oil in a wide skillet over medium heat, add the pancetta, and cook for 2 minutes, or until crisp. Set aside. Leave the fat and oil in the pan, add the sliced leeks, and cook for 3 minutes, or until soft. Add the peas for 1 minute, or until defrosted.

Carefully add the tortellini to the boiling water and cook for 3 to 4 minutes, or according to the package directions, until tender and cooked through. Drain, setting aside a scoop of pasta water.

Increase the heat under the skillet to high, pour in the wine until it mostly evaporates, about 2 minutes, then add the mascarpone, drained tortellini, and a splash of the reserved pasta water to make a loose sauce. Stir in the basil or mint leaves.

Tip the tortellini onto a large serving platter and top with the crispy pancetta. Serve.

CARAMELIZED SHALLOT & RADICCHIO BUCATINI

This bitter leaf is a staple in my refrigerator, as it's super sturdy, allowing it to sit in the refrigerator for up to a week. Keep it stored in the vegetable drawer wrapped in a damp dish towel or vegetable bag to keep it extra crisp.

SERVES : 4
PREP TIME : 12 MINS
COOK TIME : 10 MINS

14 ounces (400g) bucatini
1 head of radicchio
1 stick (110g) butter
6 banana shallots, finely sliced
2 garlic cloves, chopped
2 large handfuls of grated Parmesan
4 tablespoons pine nuts, toasted
Salt and crushed black pepper

Bring a large saucepan of salted water to a boil. Add the bucatini and cook according to the package directions. You want it al dente so consider checking it 1 minute before the directions suggest.

Shred the radicchio into thin ribbons, removing the thick core. Heat a large, heavy saucepan with 1 tablespoon of the butter. Add the sliced shallots and a pinch of salt and cook for 7 minutes, or until the shallots start to caramelize, adding more butter as you go and adding the garlic for a minute, then the radicchio.

Drain the pasta, setting aside a scant ½ cup (100ml) of the pasta water. Add the pasta to the pan and toss through the wilted radicchio. Add the reserved pasta water and the remaining butter and half the Parmesan. Toss well and stir through most of the pine nuts. Sprinkle with the remaining Parmesan and pine nuts, then season with salt and pepper. Serve.

BROTHY WONTONS WITH CRISPY SHALLOTS & CHILI SAUCE

A warm comforting bowl can sometimes be found in the unlikeliest of places … the freezer. This recipe makes the most of some ready-made frozen gyoza, some of that special chicken stock you so cleverly made ahead, as well as your trusty store of homemade chili sauce and crispy shallots you batch made at the weekend. Don't worry if you forgot to stock them as store-bought options will also work well.

SERVES : 4
PREP TIME : 5 MINS
COOK TIME : 5 MINS

- 4¼ cups (1 liter) Chicken stock (page 187)
- 4 heads of pak choi, halved
- 20 vegetable or chicken gyoza, wontons, or dumplings of your choice
- 4 tablespoons Homemade chili sauce (page 196)
- 4 tablespoons Homemade crispy shallots (page 197)

Heat the chicken stock in a large saucepan over medium heat, add the halved pak choi, and simmer for 2 minutes, then add the gyoza and cook for another 2 minutes.

Divide among bowls and top with a dollop of chili sauce and the crispy shallots. Serve at once.

OPTIONAL ADDITIONS:
Add precooked shredded chicken breast, a 6-minute jammy egg, or the soy-cured egg on page 102 also works really well here.

SPEEDY SWED-ISH WEEKNIGHT MEATBALLS

The Swedes eat meatballs with mashed potato, but I like mine with macaroni or spaghetti for a thick and creamy alternative to a classic Italian sauce; a little surprise twist for guests, as well as being speedy to make. This also works well with pickled beets, plenty of dill, and extra wholegrain mustard to really embrace those Scandi flavors.

SERVES : 4
PREP TIME : 10 MINS
COOK TIME : 15 MINS

8 thick good-quality pork sausages
Olive oil, for cooking
14 ounces (400g) pasta of choice
1 tablespoon butter
1 tablespoon all-purpose flour
¾ cup (175ml) Chicken stock (page 187)
4 tablespoons heavy cream
2 tablespoons wholegrain mustard
1 handful of chopped dill
Salt and black pepper
4 small precooked beets, chopped, for serving

Remove the sausage meat from their casings and roll the meat into 20 walnut-size pieces. Set aside.

Heat a good splash of olive oil in a large skillet over medium heat, add the sausage meat, and brown for 3 to 4 minutes until cooked through. You may have to do this in 2 batches.

Meanwhile, bring a large saucepan of salted water to a boil, add the pasta, and cook for 10 minutes, or according to the package directions until al dente.

Remove the browned meatballs from the skillet and set aside. Add the butter to the skillet and melt, then sprinkle over the flour and stir well. Cook for 2 minutes, then slowly whisk in the stock. Keep whisking until it thickens, then return the meatballs to the pan and heat through. Add the cream and mustard, then remove from the heat. Season with salt and pepper and stir in the dill. Serve the meatballs with the pasta and chopped beet stirred through.

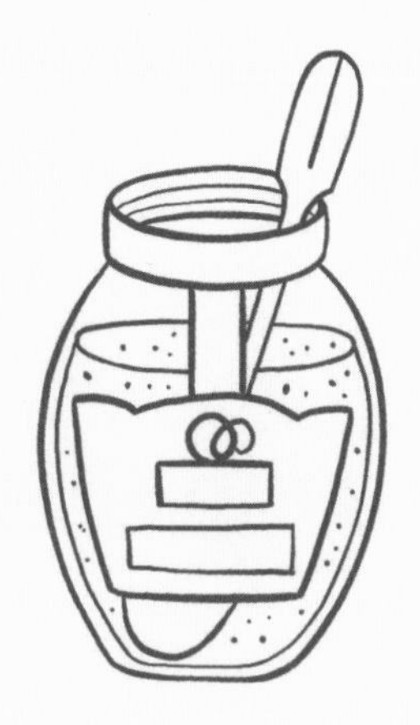

MAKE AHEAD:
You can make the meatballs and the sauce up to 3 days in advance and keep in the refrigerator, then cook the pasta when you are ready to serve and warm up the meatballs and sauce.

EASY SHRIMP, TOMATO & FETA ORZO PASTA

A pasta salad meets a risotto for this delicious, easy-to-make dinner. It's full of Mediterranean flavors and comes together in under 30 minutes. This dish also works brilliantly for an impromptu take-to-the-park picnic dinner. I love the combination of flavors—salty, sweet, and fragrant from the addition of the fennel seeds.

SERVES : 4
PREP TIME : 5 MINS
COOK TIME : 25 MINS

Olive oil, for cooking
1 onion, chopped
1 teaspoon fennel seeds
2 garlic cloves
1½ cups (300g) orzo
3 cups (750ml) vegetable stock
12 ounces (350g) peeled shrimp
1 cup (180g) sundried tomatoes
3 ounces (85g) feta, crumbled
1 handful of pitted green olives
1 handful of Italian parsley, coarsely chopped
Extra-virgin olive oil, for drizzling
Salt and black pepper
Lemon wedges, for serving

Heat a medium heavy saucepan over medium heat, add a layer of olive oil to coat, then add the onion and sweat for 5 to 7 minutes. Add the fennel seeds and garlic and cook for another 2 minutes before adding the orzo. Toast for 1 minute, then pour in the stock. Stir well, reduce the heat to low, and cook for 10 to 12 minutes, stirring constantly. Five minutes before the end of the cooking time, add the shrimp and cook until pink and cooked through.

Once the shrimp and orzo are cooked, remove the pan from the heat and add the sundried tomatoes, feta, olives, and parsley. Season with plenty of salt and pepper. Add a drizzle of extra-virgin olive oil and serve with a lemon wedge.

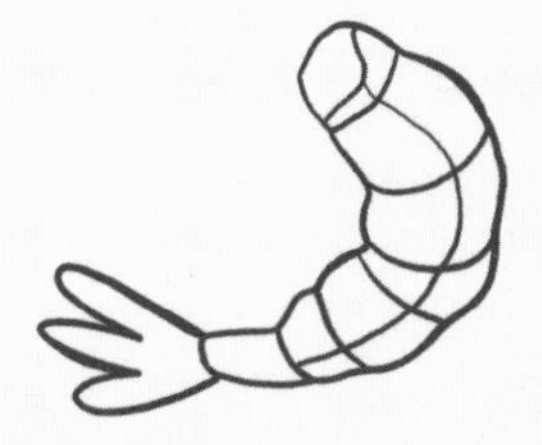

MAKE AHEAD:
I prefer to make this fresh, but it also works well at room temperature or cold as a pasta salad. It's best eaten within 1 or 2 days.

ARTICHOKE & SPINACH LASAGNA BIANCA WITH PANKO CRUMBS

This is quite fiddly for a crowd, so I think of this one as an ideal low-key dinner party dish for 2 people. An easy-to-assemble lasagna, which benefits from all the layers, but without the long cooking time. Assuming you like some crunch like me, don't worry, I've added some crispy bits to satisfy those who fight for the corner pieces.

SERVES : 2 (OR DOUBLE IT UP FOR 4)
PREP TIME : 10 MINS
COOK TIME : 10 MINS

2-ounces (55g) jarred artichokes in oil
½ cup (120ml) crème fraîche
1 teaspoon grated lemon zest
6 tablespoons grated Parmesan
8 ounces (225g) frozen spinach, defrosted
4 tablespoons panko breadcrumbs
¼ teaspoon hot pepper flakes
8 quick-cook lasagna sheets (7 ounces/200g)
Salt and black pepper

Remove the artichokes from their oil and let drain on paper towels. Heat a medium skillet with some of the oil from the artichoke jar over medium heat, add the artichokes, and fry for 2 to 3 minutes. Set aside.

Meanwhile, heat the crème fraîche in a saucepan over low heat and add the lemon zest, half the Parmesan, and plenty of cracked black pepper. Add the spinach, stir through, and keep warm over very low heat while you toast the panko crumbs and a pinch of hot pepper flakes in a dry skillet over medium heat for 1 to 2 minutes.

Bring a large saucepan of salted water to a boil. Drop in the lasagna sheets, and cook for 3 to 4 minutes, or according to the package directions until al dente, then drain.

To assemble the lasagna on individual plates, arrange a sheet of lasagna on a plate, spoon on some of the spinach and artichoke mix, then add another layer of lasagna and repeat until you have 4 layers of pasta. Finish with a sprinkle of the remaining Parmesan and the panko breadcrumbs.

MAKE AHEAD:
This lasagna is best made fresh, but can be assembled in under 10 minutes.

MIDWEEK 3-CHEESE & SPINACH SKILLET LASAGNA

This speedy béchamel cheat is so simple and decadent it will have you wondering why you ever bothered making a roux in the first place. Frozen spinach is also one of my favorite freezer-stocked ingredients for making a quick lasagna for impromptu guests.

SERVES : 4
PREP TIME : 10 MINS
COOK TIME : 30 MINS

2 pounds (900g) frozen spinach
6 ounces (or 1 x 165-g tub) cream cheese
2 eggs
¼ teaspoon ground nutmeg
1 pound (450g) crème fraîche
1¼ cups (125g) grated Parmesan
About 12 quick-cook lasagna sheets (7 ounces/200g)
1 ball mozzarella
Salt and black pepper

Preheat the oven to 400°F (200°C).

Defrost the spinach in a microwavable bowl in the microwave for 5 minutes, then press out any excess water. If you don't have a microwave, place in a heatproof bowl, pour over boiling water, and let stand for 5 to 10 minutes, then drain through a colander and press out the excess water.

Add the spinach, cream cheese, eggs, and nutmeg to a food processor and season with salt and pepper. Blend until smooth. In a separate bowl, mix the crème fraîche with half of the Parmesan and season with salt and pepper.

Spoon a third of the spinach mixture into the bottom of a 10½-inch (26-cm) ovenproof skillet, add a third of the crème fraîche, then a layer of lasagna sheets. Repeat with another layer of spinach, then crème fraîche, then lasagna. Repeat with the last third of spinach, then another layer of lasagna, and finally, add the last layer of crème fraîche over the top. Tear over the mozzarella, then finish with the remaining grated Parmesan.

Bake on the middle shelf of the oven for 25 minutes, or until it is golden and bubbling. Serve as it is or with a side salad and some garlic bread.

CHEAT'S MISO-RAMEN NOODLE BOWL WITH KIMCHI & GREENS

Having spent 2 weeks on a research trip to Japan forensically dissecting ramen and even attending a ramen school in Osaka, I'll admit this isn't altogether authentic. A couple-of-days-to-prepare ramen is wonderful to eat, but sometimes we crave a quick midweek ramen. I've added an option below for soy-cured eggs, but if you haven't got the time to make these then a 6-minute boiled egg is an excellent accompaniment.

SERVES : 4
PREP TIME : 5 MINS
COOK TIME : 20 MINS

5 cups (1.2 liters) vegetable or Chicken stock (page 187)
½ cup (40g) dried shiitake mushrooms
¾-inch (2-cm) piece of ginger, peeled and sliced
2 tablespoons red miso paste
2 tablespoons soy sauce, or to taste
9 ounces (250g) ramen noodles
Toasted sesame oil, for cooking and drizzling
1 handful of pak choi, kale, or Tuscan kale
4 to 6 tablespoons kimchi
4 Soy-cured eggs (see below) or 6-minute boiled eggs
Homemade crispy shallots (page 197), for serving (optional)

Put the stock, mushrooms, and ginger in a large saucepan and bring to a gentle simmer for 10 to 15 minutes. Stir in the miso and soy sauce and taste, adding more soy, if needed.

Cook the ramen noodles in a separate saucepan for 3 to 5 minutes, or according to the package directions.

Heat a skillet with a good splash of sesame oil, add the greens, and cook for 2 to 3 minutes until wilted. Set aside.

Add the broth to the bottom of each serving bowl, then add a nest of ramen noodles, the wilted greens, a dollop of kimchi, an egg, then drizzle with a little extra sesame oil and top with the crispy shallots, if using.

MAKE-AHEAD SOY-CURED EGGS:

- 4 eggs
- ½ cup (120ml) water
- ½ cup (120ml) soy sauce
- 2 teaspoons superfine sugar

Boil the eggs in a pan of boiling water for 7 minutes. Plunge into cold water and peel once cool. Combine the water, soy, and sugar in a narrow container and submerge the eggs in the liquid. Chill for 2 hours and up to 2 days.

CREMINI MUSHROOM, MISO & LENTIL RAGU

This umami-packed vegan dish is super handy when you need a mostly pantry solution to dinner. The miso and mushrooms come together to create a rich and almost meaty flavor, while the sunflower seeds add a pleasing crunch. If serving to cheese-eaters, I add a little grated Parmesan or pecorino, but it's just as good without.

SERVES : 4
PREP TIME : 10 MINS
COOK TIME : 40 MINS

10 ounces (270g) small cremini mushrooms
Olive oil, for cooking
2 shallots or small onions, sliced
3 plump garlic cloves, chopped
¼ cup (35g) sunflower seeds
½ cup (15g) dried porcini mushrooms
1 heaped tablespoon white miso
14 ounces (400g) cooked brown lentils
14 ounces (400g) tagliatelle or spaghetti
A few thyme leaves, for sprinkling
Grated Parmesan, for sprinkling
Salt and black pepper

Coarsely chop the cremini mushrooms into small pieces. Heat a little olive oil in a heavy nonstick skillet over low heat. Add the shallots or onions and cook for 5 minutes before adding the chopped mushrooms and garlic. Cook for 3 to 4 minutes. Reduce the heat to low, add the sunflower seeds, then cover with a lid and let the mushrooms sweat for 10 to 15 minutes.

Meanwhile, soak the dried porcini mushrooms in 1 cup (250ml) boiling water for 10 minutes.

Drain the porcini, keeping the soaking liquid. Add the porcini soaking liquid to the pan, then chop the rehydrated porcini and add them to the pan with the miso and cooked lentils. Cook for another 5 minutes. Season to taste.

If serving straight away, bring a large saucepan of salted water to a boil. Add the pasta and cook for 10 minutes, or according to the package directions until al dente. Drain the pasta, setting aside a scoop of the pasta water. Toss the pasta through the sauce, adding enough of the reserved pasta water to loosen. Divide among bowls and top with thyme and Parmesan.

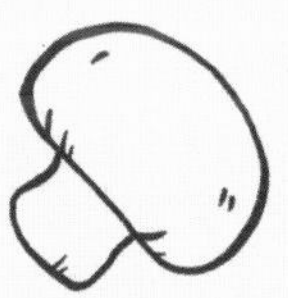

MAKE AHEAD:
Make the ragu 3 to 4 days in advance and store in the refrigerator. It also freezes well for up to 6 months.

SPICY VERMICELLI NOODLE SALAD WITH CRISPY SAUSAGE

A fiery sauce inspired by the Korean pantry staple, gochujang. This fermented spicy red chile paste adds a mega punch and depth to this dressing. I use vermicelli noodles here to make it more of a salad, but you could also serve this dish hot, stirring the vegetables through the sausage in the pan, and then serving it with egg noodles.

SERVES : 4
PREP TIME : 10 MINS
COOK TIME : 10 MINS

9 ounces (250g) vermicelli noodles
Olive oil, for cooking
8 sausages
4 carrots, julienned
4 scallions, finely sliced
2 little gem lettuce, shredded
1 handful of cilantro, leaves only
2 tablespoons sesame seeds, toasted

SESAME GOCHUJANG DRESSING:

2 tablespoons gochujang
1 tablespoon superfine sugar
2 tablespoons rice vinegar
2 tablespoons toasted sesame oil
2 tablespoons tamari
1 plump garlic clove, grated

Start by making the dressing. Mix all the ingredients together in a bowl and whisk until smooth. Set aside.

Hydrate the noodles in a heatproof bowl of boiling water for 3 to 4 minutes until soft, then drain.

Heat a large skillet over medium heat, add a splash of olive oil, then split the sausages from their casings and tear into bite-size pieces. Add to the pan and fry for 3 to 4 minutes until golden and slightly crispy. Remove the pan from the heat.

Drain the noodles and toss through the dressing, shredded vegetables, and crispy sausage. Sprinkle with cilantro leaves and toasted sesame seeds and serve on a large platter.

MAKE AHEAD:
This dressing can be made 3 to 4 days in advance. I prefer to make the rest before serving so the fresh ingredients are still crunchy.

SHEET PAN & ONE POT

SHEET PAN SEA BASS WITH FENNEL, POTATO & HOT PEPPER FLAKES

This recipe transports me to a Greek island, and while serving a whole fish might feel daunting, if you leave the filleting to your guests, most of the work is out of your hands. This is one of the few dishes in the book that serves 2 people, but you can easily adapt it to serve 4 by increasing the quantities and using a second sheet pan.

SERVES : 2
PREP TIME : 15 MINS
COOK TIME : 25 MINS

12 ounces (350g) Maris Piper potatoes, peeled
1 head fennel, shaved
1 unwaxed lemon
Extra-virgin olive oil, for drizzling
1 large sea bass, about 2 pounds (900g), cleaned
Pinch of hot pepper flakes
Salt and black pepper
Saffron aioli (page 188) or make a cheat's version (see right), for serving

Preheat the oven to 350°F (180°C).

Using a mandoline if you have one, or just a sharp knife, slice the potatoes into thin circles. Do the same with the fennel, then slice the lemon into thin circles.

Spread the potatoes, fennel, and lemon over a large sheet pan and drizzle with olive oil. Season inside the cavity of the fish, then lay over the top of the vegetables. Drizzle with olive oil and season with salt and the hot pepper flakes.

Bake in the oven for 25 minutes, or until the fish flakes away easily from the bones. Serve the fish and vegetables with a large dollop of saffron aioli.

For a cheat's version of the saffron aioli, in a heatproof bowl, add a pinch of saffron threads to 1 tablespoon of boiling water, then stir into 6 heaping tablespoons of store-bought mayonnaise with ½ grated garlic clove.

MAKE AHEAD:
You can preslice your vegetables and leave in a bowl of water, (add lemon to the fennel or it will discolor). Make sure to pat them dry with paper towels before adding to the sheet pan.

SUBS:
Any whole white fish will work well here, however, if you are using 2 smaller ones you might want to cook the vegetables for 15 minutes first.

OPINEL
INOX

DUKKAH-SPICED SCHNITZEL WITH HERB & FENNEL SALAD

I would always advise avoiding a last-minute frying session when cooking for a crowd, which is where this sheet-pan schnitzel becomes a real winner. If you can get ahead with this one, crumb coat the chicken in advance and let it chill in the refrigerator before cooking. You can do this up to a day ahead, if you prefer.

SERVES : 4
PREP TIME : 15 MINS
COOK TIME : 30 MINS

4 x 5-ounce (140-g) boneless chicken breasts, skin-on
3 tablespoons all-purpose flour
2 eggs, beaten
8 tablespoons panko breadcrumbs
3 tablespoons Dukkah (page 193)
Canola or olive oil, for drizzling
1 generous handful of herbs (page 11)
1 handful of dill pickles, chopped if large
½ head of fennel, very finely sliced
Juice of ½ lemon
1 tablespoon extra-virgin olive oil
Salt and black pepper

If you are eating the schnitzel straight away, preheat the oven to 400°F (200°C).

Remove the skin from the chicken and place the skin on a small baking sheet, sprinkle with salt, and bake in the oven for 10 minutes, or until crisp. Set the skin aside.

Sandwich the chicken breasts between 2 pieces of baking parchment and, using a rolling pin, bash them to about ¼ inch (5mm) thick. Add the flour seasoned with salt to a large plate, then add the eggs to another, and finally, add the panko bread crumbs mixed with the dukkah to a third.

Drizzle a large sheet pan (or 2—you don't want them snugly together or they won't crisp) with canola oil and heat in the oven. Dredge the pieces of chicken in the flour, then coat in the eggs, then coat in the crumbs.

Carefully remove the sheet pan from the oven and add the chicken, leaving lots of space between them to crisp. Cook for 10 minutes, then turn over and cook for another 10 minutes, or until the outside is golden and crisp and the chicken is cooked through.

Add the herbs to a salad bowl, then add the pickles and fennel, and dress with the lemon juice and extra-virgin olive oil. Season with salt and pepper. Chop the reserved chicken skin and sprinkle over the top. Serve the schnitzel with the salad on the side.

MAKE AHEAD:
You can make the schnitzel and store, covered, in the refrigerator for up to 2 days before baking.

SUBS:
This schnitzel can also be made with turkey breast, or a veal scallop. Just bash to a thin fillet in the same way as described with the chicken above.

BAKED SAFFRON & PEA RISOTTO

While I often enjoy the slow, rhythmical gesture of continuously stirring a pan of risotto, the beauty of a baked one is that it liberates me for setting the table, serving drinks, and whatever other last minute prep you might have to curtail at home.

Having a stash of frozen peas means you can make this without any fresh ingredients, but by all means add some sliced asparagus, broccoli rabe, or even ramps at the same time as the peas go in.

SERVES : 4
PREP TIME : 10 MINS
COOK TIME : 30 MINS

2 tablespoons olive oil
1 onion, finely chopped
1½ cups (285g) arborio rice
1 small glass of dry white wine (or use 3 ice cubes, page 13)
4 cups (850ml) vegetable or Chicken stock (page 187)
1 generous pinch of saffron threads
1 cup (125g) frozen peas
3 tablespoons butter
1 large handful of grated Parmesan
Salt and pepper

Preheat the oven to 375°F (190°C).

Heat a large ovenproof, heavy skillet over low heat, add the olive oil and onion, and fry for 6 to 8 minutes until the onion begins to soften. Add the rice and toast for 1 minute, stirring continuously. Add the wine and let sizzle until it evaporates. Pour in the stock and saffron and cover tightly with foil.

Bake in the oven for 15 minutes, stir, and add the peas (and any other vegetables you want to use). Cover with the foil again and return to the oven for 5 minutes. Add the butter and Parmesan, stir, and season to taste. Serve at once.

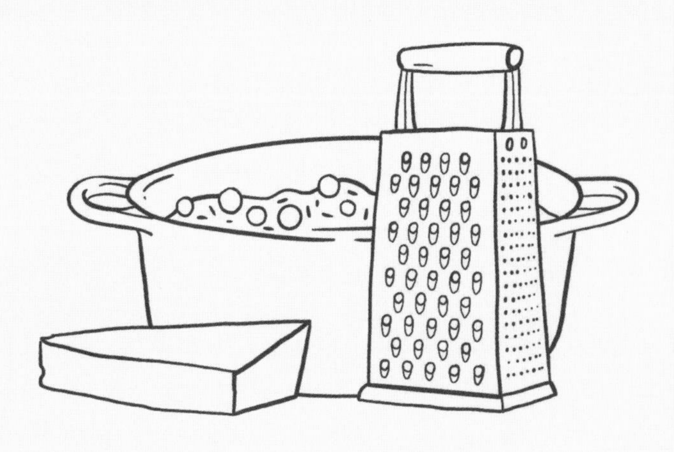

ONE-POT MISO, GARBANZO, PANCETTA & KALE STEW

Comforting and packed with umami, this rustic stew is a last-minute dinner favorite. If making this in advance, add the kale when you are reheating to keep the color a rich deep green. When it comes to the white miso paste, the saltiness can vary between brands, so I would suggest adding it 1 tablespoon at a time and tasting the broth as you go, especially as the pancetta will also season it.

SERVES : 4
PREP TIME : 10 MINS
COOK TIME : 20 MINS

Olive oil, for cooking
1 onion, finely chopped
3½ ounces (100g) pancetta, cubed
4¼ cups (1 liter) vegetable stock
1 tablespoon white miso paste
2 large handfuls of Tuscan kale, coarsely sliced
1-pound (450-g) jar garbanzo beans, drained

Heat a little olive oil in a large pot over medium heat, add the onion, and fry for 5 minutes. Add the pancetta and fry for another 2 to 3 minutes until the fat is crisping. Next, add the stock, miso, kale, and garbanzo beans. Bring to a boil then reduce the heat and simmer for 8 to 10 minutes until the kale is soft. Serve at once.

PALLARES
SOLSONA

BUTTERNUT SQUASH & SAGE TART WITH GORGONZOLA

Rich and indulgent, this quick-to-pull-together tart relies on one of my favorite refrigerator or freezer fixtures—puff pastry. This tart looks far more impressive when you serve it than it is to assemble. Once you've tried the pine nut oil for the first time, you will find yourself wanting to spoon it over everything you make.

SERVES : 4
PREP TIME : 10 MINS
COOK TIME : 30 MINS

⅔ cup (160g) crème fraîche
1 heaping tablespoon wholegrain mustard
2½ ounces (85g) gorgonzola
½ butternut squash, peeled
1 sheet puff pastry, 9 to 14 ounces/250–400g (brands vary—look for all butter)
1 small bunch of sage
Olive oil, for brushing
Black pepper
Green salad, for serving

PINE NUT OIL:
3 tablespoons pine nuts
6 tablespoons olive oil

Preheat the oven to 425°F (220°C).

Mix the crème fraîche, mustard, and gorgonzola together in a large bowl and set aside.

Slice the butternut squash thinly into circles or half-moons, depending which half of the butternut you are using.

Roll out the pastry on a counter and score a ½-inch (1-cm) border around the edge of the pastry with a sharp knife. Prick the bottom of the tart with a fork, then spoon the crème fraîche mixture onto the pastry and spread evenly across, just up to the border. Lay the butternut slices over the top, spreading them out but overlapping slightly. Tuck about 15 sage leaves between and on the butternut slices, then brush with olive oil and season with pepper.

Transfer the tart to a baking sheet and bake in the oven for 25 to 30 minutes until golden and puffy.

Meanwhile, make the pine nut oil. Toast the pine nuts in a dry skillet over low heat for 4 to 5 minutes until lightly toasted. Add the olive oil and the remaining sage to the pan and heat for 1 to 2 minutes. As soon as the tart is done, drizzle the pine nut oil over the tart and serve with a green salad.

MAKE AHEAD:
You can assemble the components for the tart in advance and store in the refrigerator, loosely covered, a day before the party, then just bake to order.

ONE-PAN ROASTED TOMATO, SPINACH & COCONUT DHAL

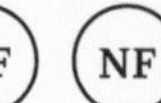

What this lacks in authenticity (purists look away now), this dhal more than makes up for in flavor and ease. A comforting winter one-pan dinner, it virtually cooks itself, to a soft and tender spiced all-in-one bowl kind of dish. If you want to keep this totally pantry-based, you could substitute the tomatoes for 2 cans of plum tomatoes.

SERVES : 4
PREP TIME : 10 MINS
COOK TIME : 40 MINS

1 red onion, thinly sliced
8 medium tomatoes, halved
5 garlic cloves, chopped
1 teaspoon ground turmeric
1½ teaspoons ground cumin
1½ teaspoons ground coriander
2 tablespoons harissa paste
1 cup (220g) red split lentils
14-ounce (400-g) can coconut milk
1½ cups (350ml) hot vegetable stock
10 ounces (280g) frozen spinach
Juice of 2 limes
salt
Homemade crispy shallots (page 197), for serving

Preheat the oven to 350°F (180°C).

Spread the onion, tomatoes, garlic, and spices, cut-side up, in a large, deep sheet pan. Brush the tomatoes with the harissa paste and season with 1 teaspoon salt. Bake for 10 minutes.

Remove the sheet pan from the oven and add the lentils, coconut milk, and stock. Return to the oven and cook for 20 minutes. Add the spinach, and cook for another 5 to 10 minutes until soft and creamy. Finish with some more salt and lots of lime juice to taste. Serve with crispy shallots.

MAKE AHEAD:
This can be made 2 to 3 days in advance and freezes very well, too.

TIP:
Try a quick little coconut condiment: Lightly toast 4 tablespoons dry shredded coconut in a small, dry skillet over low heat, then add ¼ teaspoon hot pepper flakes and a sprinkle of salt. Sprinkle over the dish to serve.

BAKED FETA WITH RADISHES, POTATO & HARISSA DRESSING

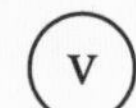

Arguably better than a perfectly crisp roast potato, these smashed potatoes become extra crunchy from their gnarly, craggy edges. The key to a really crispy potato is to only boil them for 10 to 12 minutes until they are just tender; if they are too wet they will steam too much. To make them extra crunchy, roast them for 10 minutes before adding all the remaining ingredients.

SERVES : 4
PREP TIME : 10 MINS
COOK TIME : 55 MINS

1½ pounds (700g) new baby potatoes, skin-on
7-ounce (200-g) block of feta
3 red onions, quartered (or into eighths if large)
6 garlic cloves, crushed but skin-on
1 bunch of radishes, trimmed
Olive oil, for drizzling
Salt
4 handfuls of arugula, for serving

HARISSA DRESSING:

4 tablespoons extra-virgin olive oil
2 tablespoons lemon juice
1 to 2 teaspoons harissa, to taste

Preheat the oven to 400°F (200°C).

Bring the potatoes to a boil in a saucepan of cold, salted water and boil for 10 to 12 minutes until a sharp knife is easily inserted into the center of a potato. Drain in a colander, then let dry and cool in the colander. Once cool enough to handle, crush each potato lightly with the back of a fork or a potato masher.

Transfer the potatoes to a large sheet pan with the whole feta, onions, garlic and radishes. Drizzle with oil and salt, then roast in the oven for 40 to 45 minutes until the potatoes are golden.

To make the dressing, whisk the extra-virgin olive oil, lemon juice, and harissa together in a bowl.

Serve with a handful of arugula per person and drizzle with the harissa dressing.

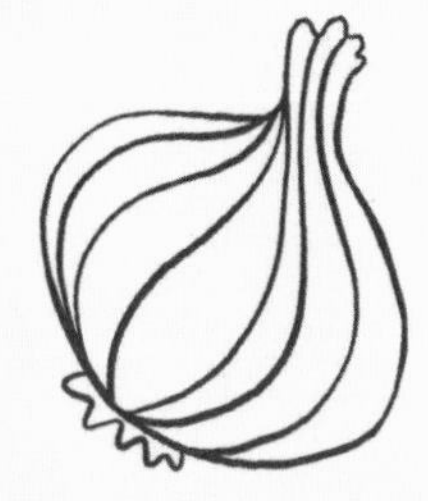

MAKE AHEAD:

You can make the dressing in advance and store in a clean jar in the refrigerator for 2 to 3 days. The dressing also works well on steamed or roasted vegetables as a side dish.

ONE-POT PASTA E CECI

A quintessential Italian peasant dish, *pasta e ceci* is truly one of the pantry greats and is a perfect dish to rustle up with what you have to hand. Jarred, rather than canned, garbanzo beans make a big flavor difference, so opt for them if you can. Any type of pasta will work well for this dish but the Italians favor short tubular ones as they are easy to coat in the thick and unctuously comforting sauce. If you have any spare Parmesan rinds in the refrigerator, then add them to the stock.

SERVES : 4
PREP TIME : 10 MINS
COOK TIME : 20 MINS

Olive oil, for cooking
6 anchovies in oil, drained
4 rosemary sprigs or use dried
5 garlic cloves, sliced
2 tablespoons tomato paste
12 ounces (350g) jarred garbanzo beans
3 cups (750ml) vegetable or Chicken stock (page 187)
7 ounces (200g) pasta (macaroni, ditalini all good here)
Grated Parmesan, for finishing (optional)
4 tablespoons pine nuts, toasted
Extra-virgin olive oil, for drizzling
Salt and black pepper

Heat a good splash of olive oil in a large heavy saucepan over low heat, add the anchovies and rosemary leaves, and sizzle for 2 to 3 minutes. Add the garlic and tomato paste and cook for another 2 minutes. Add the garbanzo beans and stock, then bring to a simmer for 5 minutes. Remove from the heat and use a handheld blender to coarsely blend about half the mixture. This will thicken the soup.

Return the pan to the heat, add the pasta, and cook over low heat for about 10 minutes (be sure to check the package directions as some shapes will vary), stirring so the pasta doesn't stick to the bottom of the pan. Season to taste.

Divide among bowls and top with Parmesan, if using, the pine nuts, and a drizzle of extra-virgin olive oil.

MAKE AHEAD:
This can be made up to the point of adding the pasta, about 2 days ahead. You may need to add some more liquid when cooking the pasta.

CHICKEN-KINDA CACCIATORE

Using a plethora of pantry staples, such as jarred roasted peppers and green olives, this is a useful one-pan dish that needs little involvement from the cook. Be sure not to overcrowd your pan too much or the juices won't reduce down.

SERVES : 4
PREP TIME : 10 MINS
COOK TIME : 50 MINS

- 4 large chicken thighs, skin-on, about 5 ounces (140g) each thigh (or 8 smaller ones)
- 2 tablespoons olive oil
- 2 red onions, sliced
- 1 bundle of thyme
- 5 garlic cloves, crushed
- 2 handfuls of pitted green olives
- 4 large roasted peppers in oil (from a 12-ounce/350-g jar)
- 14-ounce (400-g) can cherry tomatoes
- 2 x 14-ounce (400-g) cans cannellini beans, drained
- Salt and black pepper

Preheat the oven to 400°F (200°C).

Season the chicken all over. Add the olive oil to a large, heavy, ideally ovenproof, skillet, add the chicken, and sear on all sides, making sure to get the skin good and crispy over high heat. Remove from the pan and set aside on a plate.

Add the onions, thyme, and garlic to the skillet and cook over high heat for 5 minutes. Add the olives, peppers, cherry tomatoes, and cannellini beans to the pan and season well. Arrange the chicken over the top and bake in the oven for 30 to 45 minutes until the chicken is cooked through. Serve.

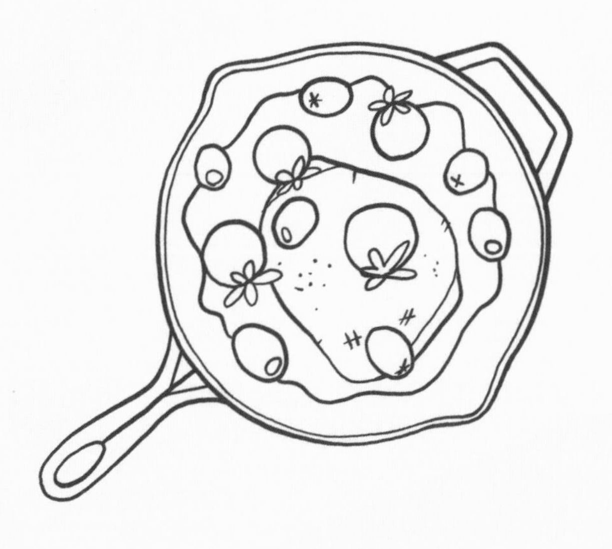

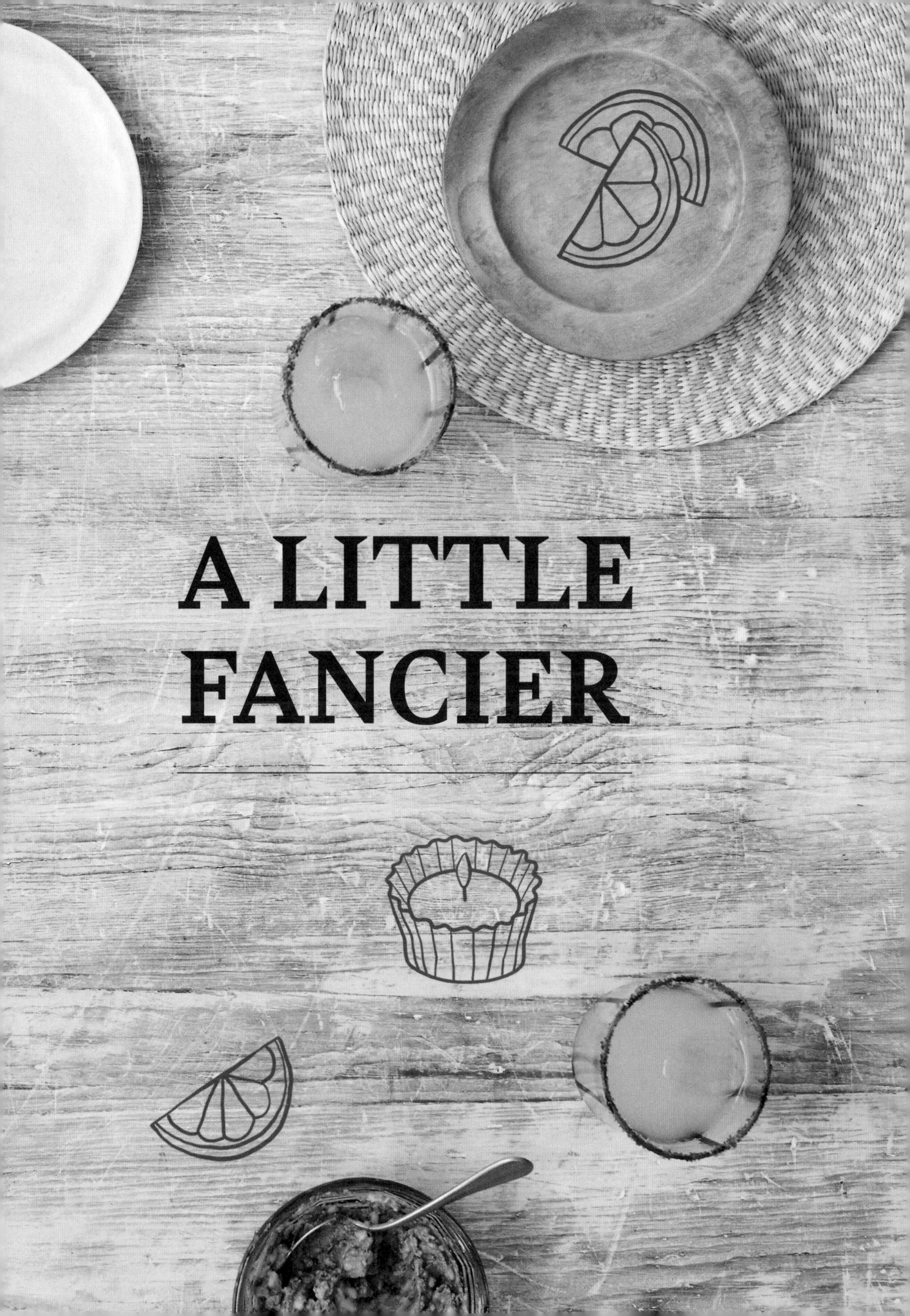

A LITTLE FANCIER

CARAMEL-GLAZED DUCK LEGS WITH PLUMS & ENDIVE

This is very loosely inspired by the flavors of a Peking dish—a rich, glossy sauce paired with dark roasted leg meat, and here, enhanced by bitter leaves and sticky sweet plums. Naturally, toasted sesame seeds are excellent on top, as is a fruity Burgundy wine to accompany it.

SERVES : 4
PREP TIME : 5 MINS
COOK TIME : 75 MINS

- 4 large duck legs, about 7½ ounces (220g) each, skin-on
- ¼ cup (50g) light brown sugar
- ¼ cup (60ml) rice vinegar
- 3 tablespoons soy sauce or tamari
- ½ stick (60g) butter
- 4 red plums, halved and pitted
- 3 tablespoons superfine sugar
- 2 tablespoons toasted sesame seeds
- 2 to 3 heads red chicory/endive or 1 head frisée salad, leaves washed and separated

Preheat the oven to 350°F (180°C).

Place the duck legs, skin-side down, in a heavy-bottomed skillet and cook over medium heat for 10 minutes, or until the skin is browned all over. You may need to do this in batches.

Combine the brown sugar, vinegar, and soy sauce in another pan. Stir, then bring to a simmer over medium heat and cook until the mixture thickens to a runny honey consistency. Set aside.

Arrange the duck on a large sheet pan, cover with foil, and cook in the oven for 40 minutes, or until tender. Increase the temperature to 400°F (200°C), remove the foil, and cook for 20 minutes, or until the legs are cooked through and the skin is crisp.

Five minutes before the duck is done, heat a large skillet with the butter over low heat until foaming. Dip the cut side of the plums into the superfine sugar and place them, cut-side down, in the butter. Cook for 3 to 4 minutes until the plums are soft and the sugar is caramelized but not burned!

Spoon a little of the caramel glaze over the duck and sprinkle with sesame seeds. Drizzle with extra plum juices and serve with the plums, chicory, and the remaining caramel glaze on the side.

MAKE AHEAD:
These duck legs work well if made in advance. If doing so, hold back some of the glaze for reheating the duck.

SUBS:
Naturally, this works very well with chicken legs too. Browning the skin will take less time than the duck as there is less fat to render.

SPATCHCOCK CHICKEN WITH SPICED BUTTER SAUCE

If you aren't already familiar with the technique of spatchcocking a chicken, then don't worry. This simple process is a brilliant trick to learn to speed up your cooking without compromising on taste. I discovered this cheat's barbecue technique when I didn't have access to an outdoor grill, but using a very hot grill pan you can achieve the high temperature char using just a conventional stove and oven.

SERVES : 4
PREP TIME : 10 MINS
COOK TIME : 35 MINS

1 good-quality chicken, about 4 pounds 8 ounces (2kg)
Olive oil, for cooking
Salt and pepper

SPICED BUTTER:

1 tablespoon butter
2 garlic cloves, finely sliced
Pinch of hot pepper flakes
⅛ teaspoon sweet smoked paprika

Preheat the oven to 400°F (200°C).

Start by spatchcocking the chicken. Place the whole chicken, breast-side down, on a cutting board, with the legs toward you. Using good scissors or poultry shears, cut along each side of the parson's nose and backbone to remove it, cutting through the rib bones as you go. Open the chicken out and turn over. Flatten the breastbone with the heel of your hand. Use 2 skewers to secure the legs and keep the chicken flat. Run the skewers diagonally through the breast and thigh meat. Rub the chicken in olive oil on both sides and season well.

Heat a large, ovenproof, preferably cast-iron grill pan (large enough to fit the chicken) over high heat. Once smoking hot, add the chicken, skin-side down, and cook for 5 to 8 minutes, searing the skin and getting a good char. Flip it over once it's golden and charred, then put it in the oven and keep cooking for another 25 minutes, or until cooked through and the juices run clear when a skewer is inserted into the thickest part of the chicken.

For the spiced butter sauce, melt the butter in a small saucepan over low heat until foaming. Add the garlic and cook for 2 minutes, or until light in color. Add the spices. Remove from the heat and pour the garlic-spiced butter over the chicken.

MAKE AHEAD:

Prepare the spatchcock chicken up to a day in advance. Season, cover with plastic wrap, and leave in the refrigerator.

CONFIT TOMATO TARTS WITH CRISPY SAGE

Squishy tomatoes combine with crispy pastry and sage to make a delicious summer dinner. You can easily double up the quantity of the tomatoes as they keep for up to 3 days in the refrigerator, then add to the top of soups, salads, or just as an accompaniment to cheese. Keep the oil for dressings.

SERVES : 4
PREP TIME : 10 MINS
COOK TIME : 40 MINS

14 ounces (400g) sweet cherry tomatoes, mix of colors
⅓ cup (75ml) olive oil, plus 1 to 2 tablespoons
4 garlic cloves, unpeeled
1 sheet puff pastry, 9 to 14 ounces/250–400g (brands vary—look for all butter)
2 teaspoons Dijon mustard
4 tablespoons grated Parmesan
12 sage leaves
Salt and black pepper

Preheat the oven to 375°F (190°C).

While the oven is heating up, place the tomatoes in a deep sheet pan that just fits them snugly, pour over the ⅓ cup (75ml) olive oil, and season. Crush the garlic in its skin and add to the sheet pan, then cook in the oven for 15 minutes. (Keep an eye on the garlic, as you want them squidgy but not colored.)

Cut the pastry into 4 x 5-inch (12-cm) circles. Use a sharp knife to make a ¼-inch (5-mm) border around the edge of the pastry and slash the inside at a diagonal. Brush the pastry with the mustard and sprinkle the Parmesan over the top. Add the confit tomatoes to the top, removing the excess oil (otherwise they risk slipping off), and tuck a now-peeled garlic clove under the tomatoes (so it doesn't burn). Bake in the oven for 20 to 25 minutes.

Heat the remaining olive oil in a small pan over medium heat until warm, add the sage leaves, and cook for 30 seconds to 1 minute until crispy. Remove the sage with a slotted spoon and drain on paper towels, then sprinkle with sea salt. Drape the sage over the cooked tarts to serve.

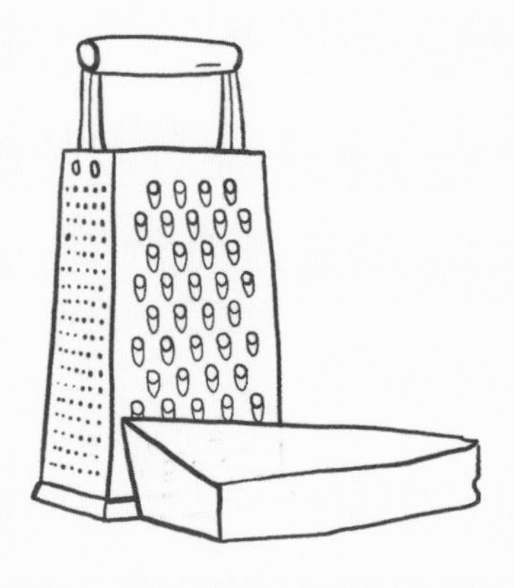

MAKE AHEAD:
Confit tomatoes can be made up to 3 days in advance, and left in the refrigerator submerged in oil. The finished tarts will sit at room temperature for a few hours, but crisp the sage before serving.

FRENCH ONION SOUP FOR FRIENDS

A pleasing pot to place in the center of the table for friends, this onion soup is a great midwinter warmer. Sweating and caramelizing the onions can't be rushed, but there's little hands-on cooking time once the onions are in the pan. This recipe transforms the humble onion from pantry essential to the supper centerstage. You can use a food processor or mandoline to finely slice the onions.

SERVES : 4
PREP TIME : 10 MINS
COOK TIME : 70 MINS

5 tablespoons butter
Olive oil, for cooking
3 pounds (1.3kg) mix of white and brown onions, thinly sliced
4 bay leaves
½ cup (20g) dried porcini mushrooms
6 garlic cloves, sliced
2 ice cubes of dry white wine (page 13) or ½ glass
2 vegetable (chicken or beef) bouillon cubes
1 teaspoon Marmite or yeast extract (optional)
½ loaf (about 6 slices) of thick sourdough bread (ideally, a couple of days old)
4 teaspoons Dijon mustard
Generous ¾ cup (100g) grated Gruyère cheese
Salt and black pepper

Heat 3 tablespoons of the butter and 3 tablespoons of olive oil in a heavy ovenproof pan with a lid over low heat until the butter has melted. Add the onions and bay leaves, season with salt, cover, and cook for 40 minutes, stirring every so often. Place the porcini mushrooms in a pitcher and pour over 2 cups (475ml) boiling water.

Add the garlic to the pan and sweat, uncovered, for another 2 to 3 minutes, scraping the bottom of the pan while letting the onions caramelize. Add the wine, then simmer for 2 to 3 minutes. Strain the porcini mushroom stock through a strainer, discarding the mushrooms (or use them in another dish). Add the stock to the pan with 3 cups (750ml) water and the bouillon cubes, and simmer for another 15 to 20 minutes. Season to taste with salt and pepper, then add the Marmite, if using.

Preheat the broiler to high. Swipe the remaining butter over the slices of bread. Add a swipe of mustard to each, then top with the grated cheese, pressing it in. Lay the slices of bread over the onions and place under the hot broiler until golden and crispy. Serve at once with plenty of pepper.

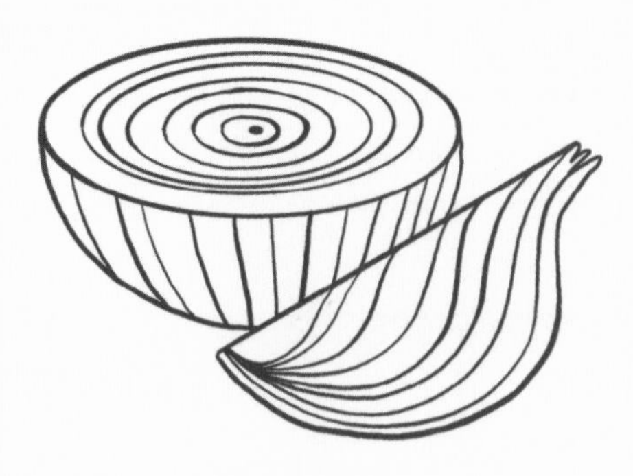

SEARED BEEF TAGLIATA WITH TONNATO SAUCE

The king of pantry sauces, this tonnato sauce is one I turn to again and again. Traditionally served with cold slices of cooked veal, I love it with seared beef with a crunchy salty crust, and some shredded radicchio wilted in the beefy juices.

SERVES : 4
PREP TIME : 10 MINS
COOK TIME : 10 MINS

2-ounce (60-g) can tuna in oil or spring water, drained
½ cup (120g) mayonnaise
3 anchovies in oil, drained
2 teaspoons lemon juice
2 tablespoons capers in brine, drained
Canola oil, for frying
4 x 6-ounce (175-g) sirloin steaks
1 large head radicchio, shredded
Salt and black pepper
Italian parsley, for serving

Start by making the tonnato sauce. Blend the drained tuna, the mayonnaise, anchovies, and lemon juice together in a food processor until smooth. Stir half the capers through, season to taste, and set aside.

Heat a good splash of oil over a cast-iron skillet over high heat. Pat the steaks dry with paper towels and season with salt and pepper on both sides. Once the pan is hot, add the steaks, 1 or 2 at a time if you have space. You want to get a really good crust on the outside so don't be afraid to do this on very high heat, and use a spatula to press it into the pan. Flip over and cook the other side. Cooking time will depend on the thickness of your steak, but I allow about 3 to 4 minutes each side, or use a thermometer to register the temperature 118°F (48°C) for rare. Repeat with the remaining steaks, then let rest.

While the steaks are resting, add the radicchio to the pan and cook in the remaining pan juices for 1 to 2 minutes until wilted.

Cut the steak into ¼-inch (5-mm) slices. Spoon the sauce onto serving plates, then serve the radicchio and the steak alongside. Sprinkle with the remaining capers and the parsley leaves.

MAKE AHEAD:
The sauce can be made 2 days in advance and stored in an airtight container in the refrigerator.

BROWN BUTTER CAULIFLOWER WITH POLENTA & SCALLOPS

Cauliflower and scallops are surprisingly delicious food friends. If you want to make your scallops extra elegant, use a sharp knife to make very fine crisscrosses over the top of each one—the little edges help the scallops get some extra browning on the outside.

SERVES : 4
PREP TIME : 10 MINS
COOK TIME : 15 MINS

1 small head cauliflower, about 1 pound (450g)
2 heaping tablespoons butter, plus 2 tablespoons, plus extra
3 cups (750ml) vegetable or Chicken stock (page 187)
1 cup (100g) quick-cook cornmeal
2 large handfuls of grated Parmesan
Olive oil, for cooking
12 scallops
Salt and black pepper

Separate the cauliflower into small florets. Add the 2 heaping tablespoons of butter to a heavy saucepan over low heat, add the cauliflower, and 2 tablespoons water. Cover with a lid and let steam and brown in the butter for about 10 minutes. Uncover, add more butter, and just let the cauliflower caramelize in the pan.

Meanwhile, bring the stock to a boil in another pan. Add the cornmeal and immediately whisk to remove any lumps. Cook for 2 to 3 minutes until smooth and hydrated. Stir through the Parmesan and lots of salt and pepper.

Heat a heavy skillet with 1 tablespoon of the remaining butter and 1 tablespoon olive oil over medium heat. Pat the scallops dry with paper towels, season with salt and pepper, and add to the hot pan. Sear on both sides for 1 to 2 minutes until pale golden on the outside and just cooked in the center (less is more here). Add the last tablespoon of butter to the pan.

Divide the cornmeal among serving plates or bowls, add the cauliflower, and serve with the seared scallops. Top with the remaining brown butter from the pan.

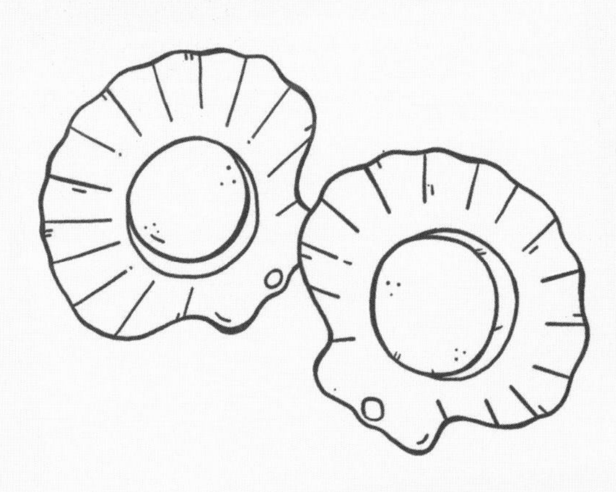

LEMON BASIL RICOTTA DUMPLINGS WITH BLISTERED TOMATOES

NF

While I'm writing this as a serving for 2 people, don't hesitate to increase the quantities for a crowd, but for me this is an ideal summery supper for 2. Use sweet, ripe tomatoes for the blistering, which will break down into a sticky concentrated tomato sauce. The dumplings will feel fragile when you are scooping them out of the bowl into the water, but the less you work them the lighter they will be in the end.

SERVES : 2
PREP TIME : 10 MINS
COOK TIME : 10 MINS

1 cup (230g) ricotta
1 egg
2 tablespoons grated Parmesan, plus extra for garnish
1 teaspoon finely grated lemon zest
4 tablespoons chopped basil, plus a little for garnish
5 to 7 tablespoons all-purpose flour
Extra-virgin olive oil, for cooking and drizzling
2 handfuls of cherry tomatoes
Salt and black pepper

Add the ricotta, egg, Parmesan, and plenty of salt and pepper to a large bowl. Add the lemon zest and stir to combine thoroughly. Stir through the basil. Add the flour and mix it lightly into the mixture. You don't want to overwork this as you want them nice and light. Start with the 5 tablespoons of flour, then add an extra 1 to 2 tablespoons if it feels like the dumplings won't form. It depends on the water content of the ricotta.

Bring a large saucepan of salted water to a boil. You are going to multitask here. At the same time, heat a decent layer of oil in a skillet over high heat. Add the dumplings to the boiling water, scooping them with 2 tablespoons (don't worry if they are a little uneven) from the bowl into the water. You will make about 10. Cook for 3 to 5 minutes until they float to the surface.

Add the tomatoes to the skillet, season, and cook for 3 to 4 minutes until they blister, the skins pop, and they release some of their juices.

Get 2 plates ready, scoop the dumplings out of the water, draining off the excess water, and divide them between the plates. Pour the tomatoes and their juices over the top, then sprinkle with a little extra Parmesan, black pepper, olive oil, and a few basil leaves.

FISH TACO PARTY

Nothing says a "relaxed" impromptu dinner party quite like a taco party. These are so easy to pull together at the last minute but just make sure you buy the best-quality breaded fish fillets or goujons available. Here, I've used cabbage as I like its crunch, but you can use shredded lettuce, carrot, or red bell pepper instead. Serve with a lime and chile salsa, a quick guacamole, and some Sriracha mayonnaise.

SERVES : 4
PREP TIME : 10 MINS
COOK TIME : 10 MINS

¼ red cabbage, shredded
Juice of 2 limes
12 to 16 frozen breaded fish fillets
12 soft white corn tortillas
Salt

QUICK GUACAMOLE:
1 avocado
½ red chile, finely chopped
Lime juice, to taste
2 tablespoons chopped cilantro

SOUR CREAM, LIME & JALAPEÑO SALSA:
6 tablespoons sour cream
2 tablespoons lime juice and zest
3 tablespoons chopped jalapeño peppers

FOR SERVING:
Pickled vegetables
Sriracha mayonnaise

For the guacamole, scoop the flesh out of the avocado into a bowl and coarsely mash. Add the chile, lime juice, and chopped cilantro and mix together until everything is combined. Set aside.

Mix all the ingredients for the sour cream salsa together in another bowl. Set aside.

Toss the shredded cabbage with the lime juice and a pinch of salt in a medium bowl, massaging the cabbage to break it down. Set aside in a serving bowl.

Cook the fish fillets according to the package directions, then heat the tortillas according to the directions on the package.

Lay out the tortillas, cabbage, breaded fish fillets, guacamole, sour cream salsa, pickled vegetables, and sriracha mayonnaise on a tray or across bowls and let everyone help themselves.

MAKE AHEAD:
Make the dips and cabbage ahead and store, covered, in the refrigerator for 2 days. Let the plastic wrap touch the guacamole so it doesn't discolor.

TIP:
If you have a gas stove, hold the tortillas with a pair of long tongs and gently char them over a low flame for an authentic, barbecued look.

TURMERIC & COCONUT FISH CURRY

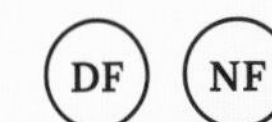

This is where you reap the rewards of that fragrant spice paste you ingeniously squirreled away in the freezer. Just stir in the spice paste, add some creamy coconut milk and lightly poached fish, and you have a delicious supper in no time at all.

SERVES : 4
PREP TIME : 10 MINS
COOK TIME : 20 MINS

Olive oil, for cooking
8 tablespoons Turmeric & ginger paste (page 190)
2 x 14-ounces (400-g) cans whole coconut milk
1 large handful of broccolini, stems and tips separated
1½ pounds (675g) skinless white fish such as hake, pollack, or cod, cut into chunks
1 handful of frozen shrimp, defrosted
2 tablespoons tamarind paste
1 teaspoon fish sauce
1 teaspoon soy sauce
Noodles or rice, for serving

Heat a medium saucepan over low heat, add a splash of olive oil and the turmeric paste, and cook for 5 minutes, stirring continuously so it doesn't catch on the bottom of the pan. Add the coconut milk and refill the can halfway with water, swirl it around, and pour it into the pan. Bring to a low simmer for 5 minutes, then add the broccolini stems and cook for another 3 minutes. Add the fish, shrimp, and broccolini tips, and cook for another 4 to 6 minutes until tender and the fish and shrimp are cooked through.

Add the tamarind paste, fish sauce, and soy sauce. Taste and add more, if needed. Serve the curry with noodles or rice.

MAKE AHEAD:
You can make the curry base 2 to 3 days in advance, but add the fish and vegetables on the evening you plan to serve it.

GLAZED BABY EGGPLANT STICKY RICE BOWLS

If you are a fan of nasu dengako, you will love this tamarind-glazed version of the famous Japanese miso-glazed eggplant dish. Tamarind is one of those instant flavor enhancers, and paired here with some sticky rice and a light cilantro salad, it is a lovely bowl of goodness.

SERVES : 4
PREP TIME : 10 MINS
COOK TIME : 25 MINS

4 tablespoons tamarind paste
4 tablespoons soft brown sugar
1 tablespoon grated ginger root
2 tablespoons finely chopped red chile
4 to 8 baby eggplants (depending on size)
2 cups (370g) sushi rice
1 teaspoon toasted sesame oil
1 handful of cilantro, leaves picked
1 tablespoon toasted sesame seeds
Pickled red onions (page 64), for serving

SUSHI RICE DRESSING:
4 tablespoons rice vinegar
4 teaspoons superfine sugar
1½ teaspoons salt

Preheat the oven to 350°F (180°C). Line a baking sheet with foil.

Mix the tamarind paste, brown sugar, ginger, and chile together in a large bowl. Halve the eggplants and score the flesh with a crisscross pattern. Add to the tamarind glaze and toss until coated, then arrange the eggplants, flesh-side up, on the lined baking sheet. Cook in the oven for 20 to 25 minutes.

Meanwhile, place the rice in a saucepan with 3 cups (700ml) cold water and bring to a low simmer. Cover with a lid and simmer for 10 minutes. When you hit 10 minutes, turn off the heat and leave the lid on for another 15 minutes to steam.

Mix all the dressing ingredients together in a bowl until the salt and sugar have dissolved. Set aside.

Add the oil to a small bowl, add the cilantro and toasted sesame seeds, and toss together until the cilantro is coated.

Toss the rice in the dressing and add to a serving bowl. Add 2 to 4 halves of the eggplants and dress with the pickled red onions, a drizzle of the remaining glaze, and the sesame cilantro salad.

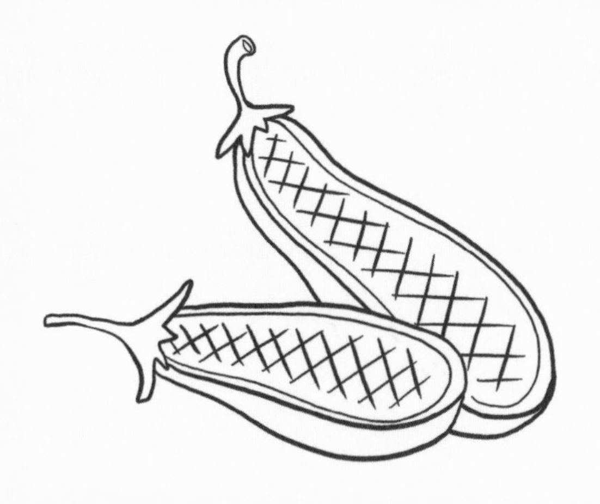

DESSERTS

SALTED CARAMEL CHEESECAKE POTS

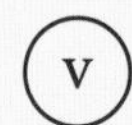

Quick to make, creamy, and indulgent, these little pots are for everyone that loves salted caramel. Buy a good-quality salted caramel for the best results. I use glasses to serve these in, but small jars or ramekins also work well. If you are an extra big fan of the salted caramel flavor profile, you could also add a pinch of sea salt flakes to the top.

SERVES : 4
PREP TIME : 10 MINS
CHILL TIME : 1 TO 2 HOURS

8 graham crackers or digestives
½ cup (120g) cream cheese
½ cup (120ml) heavy cream
3 tablespoons confectioners' sugar
4 to 6 teaspoons salted caramel (from a 7½-ounce (220-g) jar)
4 tablespoons butter

Crush the graham crackers into coarse crumbs in a bowl. I leave the odd bigger chunk for a bit of textural variation.

Whip the cream cheese, cream, and confectioners' sugar together in a large bowl until soft peaks form. Be gentle as you don't want it to get too stiff, just a light soft peak. Fold 3 teaspoons of the caramel sauce lightly through the mixture to create a ripple effect.

Melt the butter in a saucepan, pour over the crackers, and stir together. Divide the majority of the buttery crackers among the bottom of the glasses, then top with a quarter of the cheesecake mixture, then follow with another drizzle of the caramel and the remaining graham crumbs. Chill in the refrigerator for 1 to 2 hours.

MAKE AHEAD:
These little cheesecake pots are best made ahead and chilled for up to 2 days in advance.

NO-CHURN LEMON MERINGUE ICE CREAM

(V) (GF) (NF)

No ice-cream maker, no problem. This quick-to-make dessert requires less than 5 minutes' preparation, and leaves the freezer to do all the hard work. You can serve this in scoops or turn it out onto a platter and serve it in slices with fresh fruit.

SERVES : 16
PREP TIME : 10 MINS
FREEZE TIME : 5 HOURS

2 cups (600ml) heavy cream
14-ounce (390-g) can sweetened condensed milk
¾ cup (250g) lemon curd
3 large meringues (1¾ ounces/50g), crumbled

Line a 2-pound (900-g) loaf pan with plastic wrap, leaving it overhanging on all sides evenly to cover the top.

Whip the heavy cream in a large bowl until soft, light peaks form. Fold in the condensed milk, then lightly fold through the lemon curd and crumbled meringues until just mixed through.

Pour the mixture into the lined loaf pan and cover the top with the overhanging plastic wrap. Transfer to the freezer for at least 5 hours, or until set.

BAKE-TO-ORDER SALTY CHOCOLATE CHIP COOKIES

V

Take all the stress out of making an impromptu dessert by having a constant stash of bake-to-order chocolate chip cookies in the freezer at any given time. While you might be thinking "aren't cookies for kids with a cup of milk," you will be hard-pressed to find an adult that doesn't delight in a freshly made cookie.

MAKES : 14 TO 16
PREP TIME : 10 MINS
COOK TIME : 15 MINS

1 stick (115g) salted butter
½ cup (90g) dark brown sugar
½ cup (90g) superfine sugar
1 egg, plus 1 egg yolk
½ teaspoon baking powder
½ teaspoon baking soda
1½ cups (230g) all-purpose flour
1 cup (200g) chocolate chips, mix of dark and milk
Flaky sea salt

Line a sheet pan that fits in your freezer with baking parchment.

Add the butter and both sugars to a stand mixer fitted with a paddle attachment and cream together until well combined (you don't want to whisk air into it). Mix in the egg and egg yolk. In a separate bowl, measure out the dry ingredients.

Add the dry ingredients to the sugary butter and mix until combined, then scoop out with either an ice-cream scoop or a spoon into golf ball-size cookie balls and arrange on the lined sheet pan (you should have between 14 to 16). Freeze for at least 4 hours, or up to 6 months.

To bake, preheat the oven to 325°F (160°C), then sprinkle the cookies with flaky sea salt and bake for 10 to 15 minutes. The middle should still be soft but the edges firm. Leave them on the sheet pan as they cool for at least 5 minutes, as they will continue to cook. Eat when they are cool enough to handle.

MAKE AHEAD:

These will keep in the freezer for up to 6 months. Once they are frozen, take the sheet pan out of the freezer and store in an airtight container.

GRAPEFRUIT CREPES

If you don't have time to make the crepe batter, you can easily use premeasured crepe batter from a package, or even premade crepes if available in your grocery store, leaving you to just swirl over the buttery grapefruit caramel. If you are feeling particularly retro, a squirt of Chantilly cream is truly the frosting on the cake.

MAKES : 10 TO 12
PREP TIME : 10 MINS
COOK TIME : 10 MINS

1½ cups (240g) all-purpose flour
Pinch of salt
4 eggs
2 cups (475ml) whole milk
1½ sticks (175g) butter
Chantilly cream, for serving (optional)

GRAPEFRUIT CARAMEL SAUCE:

3 tablespoons superfine sugar
Juice of 2 pink grapefruit (about 1 cup/250ml juice)
1 teaspoon grapefruit zest
1 tablespoon Grand Marnier
½ stick (60g) unsalted butter, cut into small pieces

Add the flour and salt to a large bowl, make a well in the center, and break the eggs into it. Using a whisk, begin whisking the eggs. When the mixture starts to thicken, gradually add small quantities of the milk, still whisking until the batter resembles thin cream.

Melt the butter in a medium pan. Spoon 2 tablespoons of it into the batter and whisk it in, then pour the rest into a bowl and use it for frying the pancakes. Let the batter rest for at least 30 minutes.

Heat a crepe pan over medium to high heat, then reduce the heat, add some butter, swirl it round, then swirl your first ladleful of batter over the bottom of the pan. Cook for 2 to 3 minutes, flip over, and cook for another 2 to 3 minutes. Transfer to a plate and repeat until all the batter is used up.

For the sauce, tip the sugar into a nonstick skillet over low to medium heat and let the sugar melt slowly without stirring. Continue to cook until it becomes a deep, amber-colored caramel. Remove from the heat and add the grapefruit juice, zest, and Grand Marnier. Return the pan to low heat to melt the caramel into the liquid. Add the butter to the sauce, in small pieces, then bring to a boil, reduce the heat, and simmer gently until glossy and reduced slightly. Add the pancakes to the pan and warm through. Serve at once with Chantilly cream, if desired.

MAKE AHEAD:

Make this batter up to 2 days ahead and store covered in the refrigerator until ready to use. You can also make the crepes in advance, leaving a sheet of baking parchment between each one. Wrap in plastic wrap to freeze.

PISTACHIO & CANDIED ORANGE CHOCOLATE SALAME

This is the adult answer to "rocky road." You can use your Homemade candied citrus peel (page 199), or if you don't have time, then use a store-bought version or another dried fruit of your choice. You can also add a splash of Cointreau if you want to make it slightly more grownup. Needless to say, this is perfect with a short and strong coffee at the end of a dinner party.

MAKES : 1 LARGE CHOCOLATE SALAME
PREP TIME : 15 MINS
CHILL TIME : 2 TO 3 HOURS

8 graham crackers or digestives
3 x 3½-ounces (100-g) bars dark chocolate (1 chocolate orange), broken into pieces
⅓ cup (100g) light treacle
1 stick (115g) unsalted butter
½ cup (70g) pistachios
1 handful of Homemade candied citrus peel (page 199), chopped
Confectioners' sugar (optional), for dusting
Sea salt flakes

Put the graham crackers into a large bowl and crush to medium to small bite-size chunks. Find a glass bowl that fits snugly above a pan, add 1 to 2 inches (2.5 to 5cm) of water, but not so much that the water touches the bottom of the bowl. Add the chocolate, light treacle, and butter to the bowl and melt.

Remove the bowl from the heat and stir in the pistachios, chopped candied orange, and a sprinkle of salt flakes and mix to completely combine.

Lay out a large piece of plastic wrap, and evenly spoon the mixture across the center of it. Roll it up into a salame shape, twisting the ends like a candy. Let rest in the refrigerator for 2 to 3 hours until firm. Unravel and dust, if desired, with a tiny bit of confectioners' sugar so it looks even more like a salame.

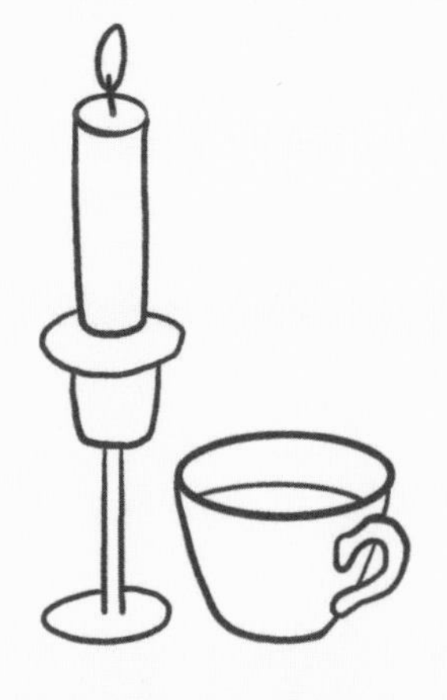

MAKE AHEAD:

You could make this chocolate salame at least a week in advance, but it's never lasted that long in my house.

FUDGY CHOCOLATE SKILLET CAKE

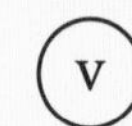

I like to think of this as the dessert version of an all-in-one pot dish. Just throw it in the skillet and serve it straight from the pan. Melting the chocolate in the pan also saves on the clearing up—just be gentle when you do melt the chocolate as it burns very easily.

SERVES : 6 TO 8
PREP TIME : 10 MINS
COOK TIME : 25 MINS

1 stick (115g) butter
⅔ cup minus 2 teaspoons (125g) superfine sugar
⅓ cup plus 2 teaspoons (75g) light brown or muscovado sugar
4½ ounces (130g) dark chocolate with at least 70% cocoa solids, broken into pieces
2 eggs
1 teaspoon vanilla extract
¾ cup (100g) all-purpose flour
½ teaspoon baking powder
1 handful of frozen strawberries
Crème fraîche or ice cream, for serving

Preheat the oven to 350°F (180°C).

Place the butter, superfine sugar, brown sugar, and chocolate in a 10½-inch (26-cm) ovenproof skillet and melt gently over very low heat, stirring until smooth. Remove the pan from the heat.

Break the eggs into a bowl and whisk with the fork. Add the eggs, vanilla, flour, and baking powder to the chocolate mixture and mix together. Dot the top with the frozen strawberries.

Bake on the middle shelf of the oven for 15 to 20 minutes until the top is set and firm but the center is still squidgy. Test this with the point of a knife.

Remove the skillet from the oven and carefully scoop it out, then serve with crème fraîche or ice cream.

ANYTHING GOES CLAFOUTIS

As simple as a crepe batter, this clafoutis is my go-to summer recipe, studded with deliciously ripe raspberries. You can, of course, replace the berries with orchard fruits, plums, or even freezer fruits—it's called an anything goes clafoutis for good reason. Serve with crème fraîche.

SERVES : 4 TO 6
PREP TIME : 10 MINS
COOK TIME : 30 MINS

1 tablespoon soft butter
10 ounces (300g) raspberries, pitted cherries/apricots/nectarines, plums, or freezer fruits, sliced
½ cup (60g) superfine sugar, plus ½ tablespoon superfine sugar
½ cup (60g) all-purpose flour
½ teaspoon baking powder
3 large eggs
1¼ cups (300ml) milk
½ teaspoon vanilla extract
Confectioners' sugar, for dusting

Preheat the oven to 350°F (180°C). Butter the inside of a 10-inch (25-cm) baking dish with the butter, then add the fruit, toss in the ½ tablespoon of superfine sugar, and cook for 5 minutes to soften. If using fresh soft berries, such as raspberries, skip this step.

Whizz the flour, baking powder, eggs, remaining superfine sugar, the milk, and vanilla in a blender or use a stick blender. Remove the dish from the oven and pour the batter over the top. Return to the oven and cook for 25 minutes, or until golden and puffy. Let cool, then dust with confectioners' sugar and serve.

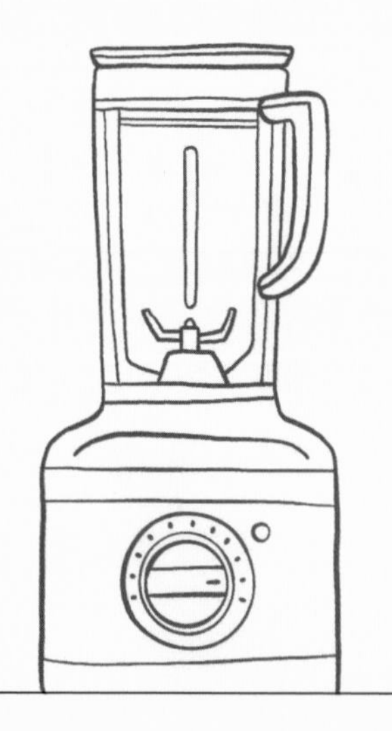

MAKE AHEAD:
Make the batter up to 2 days in advance and leave in the refrigerator.

ETON MESS TOWER

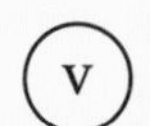

The Eton mess is the reigning champion of British desserts. Far more forgiving than a pavlova but just as delicious. Use the meringue recipe from page 198 and be generous on the fruit. The serving style here is inspired by the flamboyant "tumble" served at London restaurant Quo Vadis, but you can present it in whatever way you like.

SERVES : 4
PREP TIME : 10 MINS
COOK TIME : 0 MINS

1 pound (450g) selection of fruits: try strawberries, raspberries, blackberries, and red currants
Juice of ½ lemon
2 tablespoons superfine sugar
2½ cups (600ml) heavy cream
⅔ cup (75g) confectioners' sugar
½ teaspoon vanilla extract
6 meringues (page 198 or use store-bought)
6 generous spoonfuls of raspberry sorbet
A few edible flowers, if desired

Hull and quarter the strawberries, then add to a bowl with the other fruit and toss with the lemon juice and superfine sugar. Set aside.

Whip the cream, confectioners' sugar, and vanilla together in a large bowl with a handheld blender or electric whisk until soft peaks form. This will keep chilled for a few hours.

Break the meringues in half and pile them up into a pyramid on a large serving plate, dolloping the whipped cream, sorbet, and fruit between them—imagine they are the cement holding it all together. Add a few flowers to decorate and serve.

MAKE AHEAD:
All the components of this dessert can be made in advance, then piled together at the last minute before serving.

SUBS:
I've opted for red fruits like strawberries and raspberries, but a tropical mix of mango, passion fruit, lime juice, and papaya is excellent, too.

ROSÉ SGROPPINO

Is it a cocktail, a palate cleanser, or a dessert? I like to serve this in Marie Antoinette-esque coupe glasses to look extra elegant. Be sure to start with very cold wine and very cold vodka. In lieu of the blender, this can also be made to a firmer, less frothy texture using a hand whisk.

SERVES : 4 TO 6
PREP TIME : 5 MINS

11 ounces (310g) lemon sorbet
3½ ounces (100ml) vodka
7 ounces (200ml) rosé frizzante/prosecco

Put the sorbet, vodka, and prosecco into a large bowl. Using a stick blender, completely combine everything together to create a smooth, creamy, foamy consistency. Transfer to a pitcher and divide among 4 to 6 glasses. Serve.

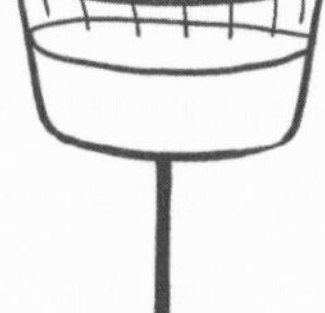

TIP

This also works well as a boozy frozen sorbet. Simply pour into an airtight container and freeze for 3 to 4 hours, then scoop out.

RASPBERRY SORBET BAKED ALASKA

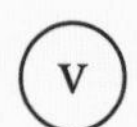

A cheat's dessert that looks very impressive, this baked Alaska is easy to assemble, but does require a small last minute step. Prescooping your sorbet ahead of serving is a great food styling trick. You can scoop when your sorbet is the perfect temperature, then just have the balls waiting in the freezer for when you are ready to serve. Using the meringue make-ahead method on page 198 is the final step for a beautiful snowy white peak.

SERVES : 4
PREP TIME : 15 MINS
FREEZE TIME : 60 MINS

4 large scoops of raspberry sorbet
1 small store-bought cake, about 1 pound (450g) (anything light works well, chocolate is good)
2-egg meringue (page 198)

Pre-scoop your sorbet and freeze for at least 1 hour.

Slice the cake into 4 x 1-inch (2.5-cm) thick pieces, then cut them out into 3-inch (7.5-cm) circles. Cover and set aside. You can do this in the morning of the dinner party, but just be sure to store them in an airtight container so they don't dry out.

Just before serving, set aside 10 minutes to do the final meringue topping. For the meringue, use the method on page 198 to make the soft meringue, but don't bake it. Instead, scoop it into a pastry bag, if you want to be neat, or just leave it in the bowl.

Assemble a scoop of sorbet on each cake base, then use a palette knife or the back of a spoon to spread the meringue all around the sorbet and cake. If you are feeling extra fancy, use a pastry bag fitted with a star nozzle to pipe little stars of meringue all over the surface. Use a blowtorch to lightly scorch the side of the meringue and serve at once.

MAKE AHEAD:
Make the scoops of raspberry sorbet as soon as you get home from the store and it's likely to be the perfect scoopable texture. Line a baking sheet (that fits in your freezer) with foil. Use an ice-cream scoop to make 4 large scoops of sorbet and press them into the sheet so the top is round and the base is slightly flat. Freeze for 2 to 3 hours, or up to 3 months

MACERATED BERRY MISÙ

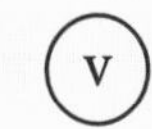

When it's strawberry season there's nothing more appealing for me than a bowl of strawberries bathing in their own jazzed-up juices. Toasted fennel seeds, tossed through the cut strawberries and then left to steep, is just a little tweak that makes this very simple dish feel that bit more "dinner party." The addition of crushed savoiardi ladyfingers and cream hints to everyone's favorite Italian trattoria dessert.

MAKES : 4
PREP TIME : 10 MINS
STEEP TIME : 30 MINS

14 ounces (400g) strawberries
3 tablespoons lemon juice
1½ tablespoons granulated sugar
1½ teaspoons fennel seeds
6 to 8 savoiardi ladyfingers
1¼ cups (300ml) heavy cream
3 to 4 tablespoons confectioners' sugar
Splash of dark rum

Hull and halve the strawberries, or quarter them if they are large. Add them to a bowl, then stir through the lemon juice and granulated sugar. Toast the fennel seeds in a dry skillet over low heat for 1 minute, then pour over the strawberries and toss them through. Let steep for at least 30 minutes.

Place the savoiardi in a large bowl and crush with the back of a rolling pin, creating a mix of big crumbs and some fine ones.

In a separate bowl, whip the heavy cream and confectioners' sugar together. Stir through most of the crushed savoiardi and add the splash of rum.

Layer up the desserts in 4 serving bowls or sundae glasses, starting with a few spoonfuls of the strawberries in the bottom, then adding a dollop of cream, and repeating. Finish with a few extra crushed pieces of savoiardi.

BRIOCHE PAIN PERDU WITH MANGO FRO-YO

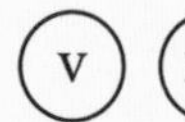

You might know this better as French toast, but call it "pain perdu," serve it as a dainty portion, and suddenly you've got yourself a lavish French dessert. By changing the portion size and serving it with a very speedy homemade fro-yo, this dessert becomes slightly more elegant and little less "brunch."

SERVES : 4
PREP TIME : 5 MINS
COOK TIME : 5 MINS

1 small loaf brioche bread, about 1 pound (450g), ideally a couple of days old
2 eggs
½ cup (120ml) whole milk
½ teaspoon vanilla bean paste
½ stick (60g) butter
3 tablespoons superfine sugar
10 ounces (300g) frozen mango pieces
4 tablespoons plain Greek yogurt
1 to 2 tablespoons lime juice
2 to 3 tablespoons maple syrup, for drizzling

Slice the crusts off the brioche, then cut the bread into 1-inch (2.5-cm) slices. Set aside.

Whisk the eggs, milk, and vanilla together in a large bowl. Heat a large nonstick skillet with 2 tablespoons of the butter over low heat until foamy. Dip the brioche slices into the egg mixture, then add the brioche slices, in batches, to the skillet. Cook for 1 to 2 minutes on each side, or until golden, then sprinkle the slices with sugar and toss once more in the pan to caramelize. Transfer to a plate and repeat with the remaining brioche slices and butter.

For the mango fro-yo, whizz the frozen mango, yogurt, and lime juice together in a food processor.

Serve the brioche, drizzled with maple syrup and the mango fro-yo on the side .

SUBS:

You can substitute the mango fro-yo for a store-bought version, if desired.

EASY FRUITY JAM TARTS

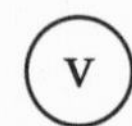

The simplest but the sweetest of tarts, these are a summertime favorite of mine. Like the Anything goes clafoutis, on page 170, this is another dessert where most seasonal fruits will work well, but when apricots or strawberries are at their peak, these are sublime. Use the strawberry jam for the strawberries and likewise for the apricot. Serve them with a dollop of crème fraîche or vanilla ice cream.

MAKES : 4
PREP TIME : 10 MINS
COOK TIME : 20 MINS

- 1 sheet puff pastry, 9 to 14 ounces/250–400g (brands vary—look for all butter)
- 4 tablespoons strawberry or apricot jam
- 16 strawberries and 4 largeish apricots or 4 nectarines

Preheat the oven to 375°F (190°C). Line a large sheet pan or baking sheet with baking parchment.

Roll the puff pastry out on a counter until it is about 1/32 to 1/16 inches (1 to 2mm) thick, then cut the pastry into four 3 x 5-inch (7.5 x 13-cm) rectangles. Use a sharp knife to make a ¼-inch (5-mm) border around the edge of the pastry and slash the inside at a diagonal. Spoon 1 tablespoon of jam per tart into the center of the pastry and spread out, leaving the border clear. Cut the fruits into slices and arrange the fruits on top of the jam.

Transfer the jam tarts to the lined baking sheet and bake in the oven for 20 minutes, or until golden and crisp.

MAKE AHEAD:
Make these tarts a few hours before serving, but leave at room temperature as they become dense when refrigerated.

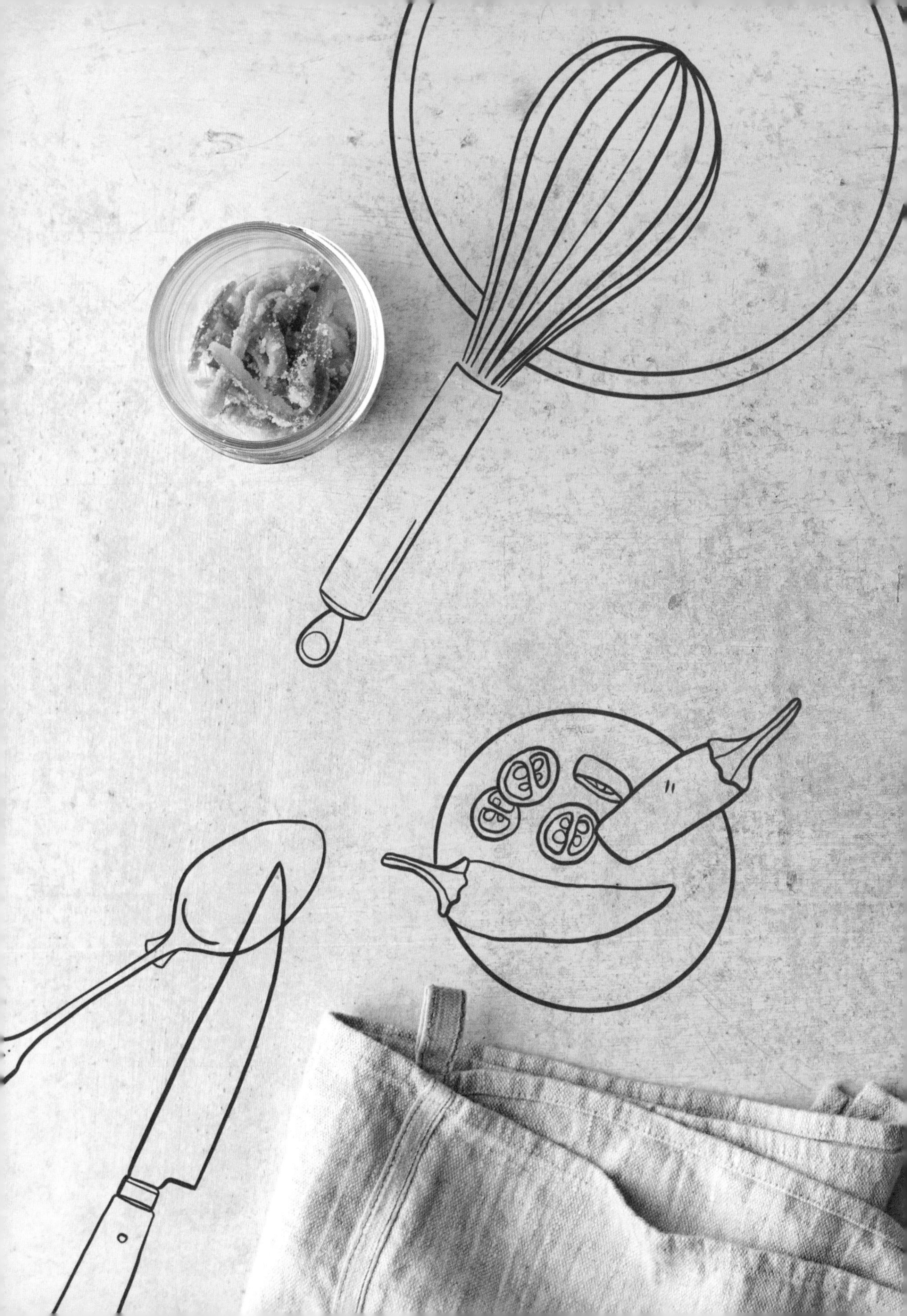

MAKE AHEAD

MAKE-AHEAD CHICKEN STOCK

There's no exact science to chicken stock—sometimes you might be making it from odds and ends of chicken bones left over from your Spatchcock chicken (page 143); other times you might be batch packing your freezer after a visit to the store. If I'm making stock without a leftover carcass I tend to choose wings, as they are both affordable and contain more collagen than other parts, resulting in a richer texture.

MAKES : 6 CUPS (1.5 LITERS)
PREP TIME : 10 MINS
COOK TIME : 2 TO 3 HOURS

3 pounds (1.3kg) chicken carcasses or wings, etc.
1 carrot
1 onion
2 bay leaves
2 celery stalks
1 teaspoon black peppercorns
Salt

Place all the chicken pieces and bones, 2 quarts (1.9 liters) water, the vegetables, bay leaves, and peppercorns in a large stockpot with a pinch of salt. Bring to a boil, skimming the surface with a slotted spoon, then turn the heat down to a very gentle simmer and simmer for 2 to 3 hours. Strain the stock through a strainer, discarding the solids, then let the stock cool. Transfer to an airtight container and store in the refrigerator or freezer.

MAKE AHEAD:
This stock keeps for 3 to 4 days in the refrigerator or up to 6 months in the freezer. You can store it in separate airtight containers, or even ice-cube trays, so then you don't have to defrost a lot for a small portion.

MAYONNAISE

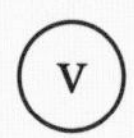   

A store-bought mayonnaise is versatile, but nothing will ever quite match up with a homemade version. Make at the weekend and have it ready to serve with fish or as a dip in the week. If your mayonnaise splits (goes from thick to liquid), then all is not lost. Whisk an egg yolk, then start gradually incorporating the split mayonnaise into the egg yolk.

MAKES : ABOUT 1 CUP (250ML)
PREP TIME : 5 MINS
COOK TIME : 0 MINS

2 egg yolks
1 teaspoon Dijon mustard
1 cup (250ml) mild flavored oil (I use a mix of olive and vegetable)
1 teaspoon lemon juice
Salt and black pepper

Add the egg yolks to a large bowl, then add the mustard and whisk until well combined. Start adding the oil in a slow, steady stream, whisking vigorously between each addition. Keep adding the oil, until you are happy with the consistency, then taste. Add the lemon juice at the end and season to taste. Serve or store in the refrigerator in an airtight container for 5 to 7 days.

SAFFRON AIOLI

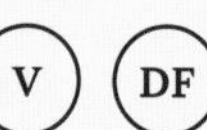   

Generous pinch of saffron threads

Use the basic mayonnaise recipe above, but start with the saffron. In a small bowl, infuse the saffron in 1 tablespoon boiling water for 10 minutes, then add to the thickened mayonnaise.

LEMON AIOLI

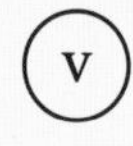   

1 (or 2) small garlic clove(s), grated
½ teaspoon Dijon mustard
2 egg yolks
Scant 1 cup (200ml) vegetable oil
Juice of ½ lemon

Add the grated garlic to a large bowl with the mustard, then add the egg yolks. Whisk together, then add the oil, about 1 tablespoon at a time, whisking well in between each addition until it is thick and unctuous. Stir in the lemon juice, then let chill until ready to use. Store in an airtight container in the refrigerator for 5 to 7 days.

2 FRAGRANT PASTES FOR ALL PURPOSES

Making some spice pastes ahead of time is one thing you will never regret. You can store these pastes in ice-cube trays in the freezer for up to 6 months, then add them to your dish when you need them.

LEMONGRASS & CILANTRO PASTE

GF

MAKES : 1 CUP (250G)
PREP TIME : 5 MINS
COOK TIME : 0 MINS

5 garlic cloves, peeled
2-inch (5-cm) piece of ginger, peeled
3 lemongrass stalks, outer leaves peeled, coarsely chopped
2 green chiles
A large handful of basil (20g), plus extra
A bunch of cilantro (30g), plus extra

Blend all the ingredients together in a blender or food processor until smooth. Loosen with 2 tablespoons water. Use at once or store in an airtight container for 3 days in the refrigerator or for up to 6 months in the freezer.

Use this paste to make the Spiced paneer and garbanzo bean curry on page 69.

TURMERIC & GINGER PASTE

MAKES : 1 CUP (250G)
PREP TIME : 5 MINS
COOK TIME : 0 MINS

4 lemongrass stalks
1-inch (2.5-cm) piece of ginger
5 red chiles
4 garlic cloves
2 red onions
Juice of 3 limes
2 teaspoons ground turmeric

Blend all the ingredients, except the turmeric, together in a blender or food processor until smooth. Loosen with 2 tablespoons water. Add the turmeric at the end (to save your blender from overexposure). Use at once or store in an airtight container for 3 days in the refrigerator or for up to 6 months in the freezer.

Use this paste to make the marinated Broiled chicken skewers on page 75.

DUKKAH

VG DF 

MAKES : 8 OUNCES (200G)
PREP TIME : 5 MINS
COOK TIME : 15 MINS

- 3½ ounces (100g) blanched hazelnuts
- 1 ounce (30g) slivered almonds
- 5 tablespoons sesame seeds
- 1½ tablespoons coriander seeds
- 1½ tablespoons cumin seeds
- 3 teaspoons flaky sea salt

Dukkah is a Middle Eastern spiced nut and seed blend that is a permanent fixture in my pantry. Use it to sprinkle over salads, pep up some tomatoes on toast, or even use to coat the sheet pan schnitzel (page 115). I've used hazelnuts and almonds in this mix, but you can use other varieties of nuts, if you prefer.

Toasting the nuts in the oven gives them a more even golden brown color and there's also less chance of burning. If you have stored this for a while in an airtight jar, you can lightly retoast it in a skillet to give it an aroma boost.

Preheat the oven to 300°F (150°C).

Spread the hazelnuts out over a baking sheet and toast in the oven for 10 minutes, or until golden, adding the slivered almonds after 5 minutes. Keep a good eye on them as they can burn easily. You want them a pale golden brown. Decant them into a bowl.

Toast the sesame seeds in a dry pan on the stove until lightly golden, then decant them into the bowl with the nuts. Add the coriander and cumin seeds to the same pan and toast for 1 minute, or until fragrant. Add to the bowl. Pulse or bash half of the mixture in a food processor or mortar and pestle, then return it to the bowl with the salt and mix everything together. Store in an airtight container or jar in a cool place indefinitely.

EVERYTHING BAGEL SEASONING

VG DF GF NF

MAKES : ½ CUP (120G)
PREP TIME : 5 MINS
COOK TIME : 0 MINS

- 2 tablespoons poppy seeds
- 1 tablespoon white sesame seeds
- 1 tablespoon black sesame seeds
- 1 tablespoon dried garlic granules
- 1 tablespoon plus 1 teaspoon dried onion granules
- 1 teaspoon toasted nori flakes
- 2 teaspoons flaky sea salt

This seasoning first came to my attention on a savory cream cheese croissant I bought at a London bakery and it has since has become a firm favorite of mine.

Combine the poppy seeds, sesame seeds, dried garlic, dried onion, nori, and salt together in a large bowl and stir until well combined. Store in an airtight jar or container in a cool place for 6 months.

MY FAVORITE VINAIGRETTE

Store this vinaigrette in a jar in your refrigerator and you will have a side salad ready to go in minutes. But don't forget, dressings aren't just for salads—toss through warm green beans, asparagus, and broccoli spears. When buying a head of lettuce, separate and wash the leaves thoroughly, dry them in a salad spinner, and store in the spinner in the refrigerator. The leaves will remain crisp and fresh for up to 4 days.

MAKES : 1 PORTION (FOR ABOUT A 4-PERSON SALAD)
PREP TIME : 5 MINS
COOK TIME : 0 MINS

2 tablespoons white wine, red wine, or apple cider vinegar
2 teaspoons Dijon mustard
A good pinch of salt
3 tablespoons olive oil
Black pepper

In a bowl (a big salad bowl if you are about to eat it straightaway), whisk the vinegar, mustard, and salt together until well combined. Add the olive oil, 1 tablespoon at a time, whisking as you go until it is thick. If you have mixed this in the salad bowl, add the washed leaves and toss them gently with clean hands (the best way to ensure you don't damage the leaves) until they are coated in the dressing. Season with cracked black pepper.

MAKE AHEAD:
Make a large batch and store it in a jar, then remove from the refrigerator 30 minutes before using, giving it a good shake as the oil will have solidified.

A FEW VARIATIONS:

- Add 1 tablespoon finely chopped herbs
- Try a version with wholegrain mustard
- Swap out the vinegar for fresh lemon juice for a really zingy dressing
- Grate in a little fresh garlic for a punch
- Add a chopped hard-boiled egg, 1 teaspoon capers, and 1 tablespoon chopped gherkins for a little gribiche dressing
- Add 1 to 2 teaspoons honey if you are serving bitter leaves
- Anchovies are always a good idea!

HOMEMADE CHILI SAUCE

This is my go-to chili sauce. You can make this up to a week ahead, but it rarely lasts for longer than a couple of days in my refrigerator. I use it for drizzling, dipping, or dolloping onto all types of dishes. Try it on the smashed cucumber salad (page 58) or the brothy wontons (page 93).

MAKES : ABOUT 1 CUP (250ML)
PREP TIME : 5 MINS
COOK TIME : 5 MINS

4½ ounces (120g) or about 8 large red chiles, chopped
4 garlic cloves, chopped
2-inch (5-cm) piece of ginger, peeled and chopped
¼ cup (60ml) vegetable oil
1 tablespoon soft brown sugar
2 tablespoons light soy sauce

Put the chopped chiles, garlic, and ginger into a food processor and blend until it is a rough paste. Heat the oil in a small saucepan over medium-high heat, add the paste, and cook for 3 to 4 minutes to soften. Stir through the sugar and cook for 1 minute before stirring through the soy sauce. Remove the pan from the heat and let cool, then transfer to a clean jar or airtight container and store in the refrigerator for up to a week.

HOMEMADE CRISPY SHALLOTS

Crispy shallots are one of my favorite items to stock in the pantry, and they are added to a number of recipes in this book, such as the Cheat's miso-ramen noodle bowl (page 102). They provide the most perfect crunch for all sorts of dishes, and the oil left behind in the frying process gets gently infused with the aroma from the shallots, which you can use for dressings, frying eggs, or stir-frying.

MAKES : A FEW HANDFULS
PREP TIME : 5 MINS
COOK TIME : 10 MINS

1 cup (250ml) vegetable oil
1 pound (450g) banana shallots, sliced
Sea salt

Line a rimmed baking sheet with paper towels and suspend a fine-mesh strainer over a bowl.

Heat the oil in a heavy-bottomed pan over medium heat, add the sliced shallots, and cook for 6 to 8 minutes. Keep a really close eye on these, as they will take a good 5 minutes to get going but you want to be very vigilant as they can turn from lightly amber to burned extremely quickly, which makes them quite bitter! Move the shallots around as they cook (long chef's tweezers are great for the job), and don't take your eyes off them. Once they are golden, quickly strain through the strainer set over the bowl as they will keep cooking. Transfer the drained shallots to the lined baking sheet and sprinkle with lots of sea salt. Strain the infused oil into a clean jar to reuse for frying eggs, stir-fries, more fried shallots, etc.

Store the crispy shallots in an airtight container lined with paper towels for up to a month.

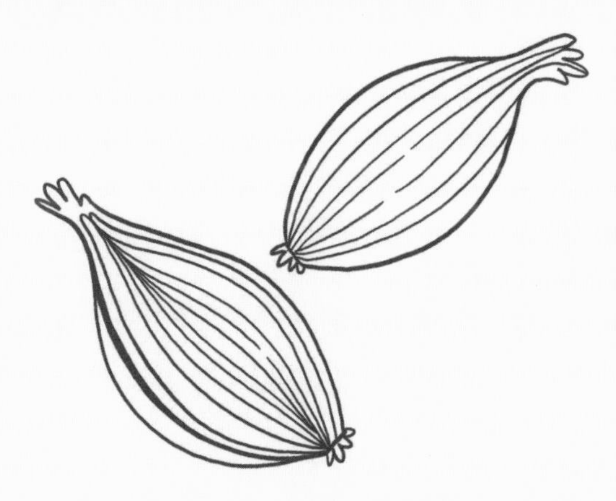

HOMEMADE MERINGUE

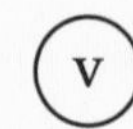

Meringues are an excellent way to use up those leftover egg whites from making Mayonnaise (page 188). Homemade meringues are easy to make and store so they are great for impromptu desserts, such as the Eton mess tower (page 173). Or use this technique for the Raspberry sorbet baked Alaska (page 176). Use at least 2 egg whites or make a large batch with 4 or 5. I've given the ratios, so just scale it up to suit.

PREP TIME : 10 MINS
COOK TIME : 2 HOURS

2 ounces (about 60g) superfine sugar per egg white
1 egg white

Preheat the oven to 375°F (190°C). Line a large baking sheet with baking parchment. Add the sugar to the baking sheet and heat in the oven for 5 to 8 minutes until the sugar is just starting to melt at the edges. Reduce the oven temperature to 200°F (100°C) and leave the door open to help the oven cool down quickly.

Whisk the egg white in a stand mixer fitted with a whisk attachment until frothy, then start to incorporate the hot sugar, 1 tablespoon at a time, whisking continuously on high speed. Once all the sugar is incorporated, keep whisking as the mixture cools down, scraping down the edges of the bowl with a rubber spatula in case any of the sugar has escaped. You can pinch a bit of the mixture and rub it between your fingers to check if the sugar has dissolved. Keep whisking if it hasn't.

Line a sheet pan with baking parchment, then dollop mounds of meringue on top leaving a few inches of space in between for the air to circulate. Check that the temperature of the oven is low, then add the meringues and bake for 2 hours, or until dry and they easily come away from the bottom of the pan.

MAKE AHEAD:
These meringues will keep in an airtight container for up to 2 weeks or up to 3 months in the freezer.

HOMEMADE CANDIED CITRUS PEEL

This candied citrus peel is a simple end to a meal with a strong espresso, but it is also a versatile addition to desserts, or chopped over ice cream. I used it for the Pistachio & candied orange chocolate salame (page 165), but it would also work well just dipped in melted dark chocolate, or chopped into the no-churn ice cream on page 159.

MAKES : 2 BIG HANDFULS
PREP TIME : 5 MINS
COOK TIME : 35 MINS

2 large oranges
2 cups (400g) superfine sugar, plus ½ cup (100g) for dusting

To remove the skin from the oranges, trim ½ inch (1cm) off the top and bottom of the orange, then slice through the skin in quarters and peel away from the flesh Slice into long pieces. Place in a large saucepan of cold water and bring to a simmer. Simmer for 10 minutes. Drain and repeat this process one more time.

Place the sugar and 2 cups (475ml) water in another large pan and bring to a simmer to dissolve the sugar.

Add the orange peel to the syrup and simmer for 30 minutes. Using a slotted spoon or colander, drain the peel from the syrup (keep the syrup for making cocktails), then lay the orange pieces out over a baking sheet in a single layer and cover with a heavy dusting of sugar. Let stand for 2 days.

Store in an airtight container for about 6 months, well coated in sugar. If the sugar gets humid, tip it away and replace.

MENU PLANNER

SPRING

DRINKS & NIBBLES
Gilda pinxto with Hemingway Daiquiri (page 20)

APPETIZER
White asparagus vichyssoise (page 62)

ENTREE
Sheet pan sea bass with fennel, potato & chile (page 112)

DESSERT
No-churn lemon meringue ice cream (page 159)

SUMMER

DRINKS & NIBBLES
Slivered melon & prosciutto with Margaritas (page 24)

APPETIZER
Spanish tomato soup with serrano ham crisp (page 61)

ENTREE
Easy shrimp, tomato & feta orzo pasta (page 96)

DESSERT
Eton mess tower (page 173)

FALL

DRINKS & NIBBLES
Stracciatella, anchovy & fried sage bruschetta (page 27)

APPETIZER
Wedge salad & blue cheese dressing (page 64)

ENTREE
Creamy tortellini with pancetta, peas & leeks (page 88)

DESSERT
Grapefruit crepes (page 162)

WINTER

DRINKS & NIBBLES
3-ingredient whipped feta dip with iced tea (page 32)

APPETIZER
Crispy gyoza salad with a zippy Thai-style dressing (page 52)

ENTREE
Caramel-glazed duck legs with plums & endive (page 132)

DESSERT
Salted caramel cheesecake pots (page 156)

READY IN AN HOUR

APPETIZER
Wedge salad & blue cheese dressing (page 64)

ENTREE
Seared beef tagliata with tonnato sauce (page 140)

DESSERT
Raspberry sorbet baked Alaska (page 176)

APPETIZER
Phyllo-fried feta with a tomato-caper salad (page 50)

ENTREE
Salmon with herby crème fraîche (page 76)

DESSERT
Easy fruity jam tarts (page 182)

VEGETARIAN

DRINKS & NIBBLES
Artichoke, lemon & ricotta bruschetta (page 27)

APPETIZER
Watermelon, salted ricotta & mint salad (page 56)

ENTREE
Skillet fried gnocchi with wild mushrooms (page 82)

DESSERT
Brioche pain perdu with mango fro-yo (page 180)

VEGAN

DRINKS & NIBBLES
5-minute crispy farinata with Bloody Mary (page 18)

APPETIZER
Asparagus with creamy almond tarator (page 49)

ENTREE
One-pan roasted tomato, spinach & coconut dhal (page 122)

DESSERT
Pistachio salame (use vegan chocolate) (page 165)

SPANISH-STYLE SUPPER

DRINKS & NIBBLES
"Pan con tomate" bruschetta (page 26)

APPETIZER
Spanish tomato soup with serrano ham crisp (page 61)

ENTREE
Chicken kinda-cacciatore (page 128)

DESSERT
Salty chocolate chip cookies (page 160)

ITALIAN-INSPIRED FEAST

DRINKS & NIBBLES
Figs with gorgonzola with sage & citrus spritz (page 31)

APPETIZER
Burrata with beet & grated tomato (page 55)

ENTREE
Caramelized shallot & radicchio bucatini (page 90)

DESSERT
Rosé sgroppino (page 174)

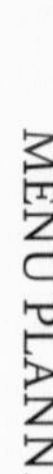

MENU PLANNER

ALL THE FAMILY

DRINKS & NIBBLES
Mediterranean mezze platter (page 39)

ENTREE
Fish taco party (page 148)

DESSERT
Eton mess tower (page 173)

SPICE DRAWER FAVORITES

APPETIZER
Smashed cucumber, sesame & cilantro salad (page 58)

ENTREE
Spiced butter eggs with lentils & crispy shallots (page 72)

DESSERT
Macerated berries misù (page 179)

PANTRY HEROES

DRINKS & NIBBLES
5-minute crispy farinata with Bloody Marys (page 18)

ENTREE
One-pot pasta e ceci (page 127)

DESSERT
Pistachio salame (page 165)

KIDS' FRIENDS' DINNER

DRINKS & NIBBLES
Chile jam twists & Hibsicus coolers (page 34)

APPETIZER
Spanish tomato soup with serrano ham crisp (page 61)

ENTREE
Chicken-kinda cacciatore (page 128)

COCKTAIL HOUR

DRINKS & NIBBLES
Gilda pinxto with Hemingway Daiquiri (page 20)

APPETIZER
Asparagus with creamy almond tarator (page 49)

DRINKS & NIBBLES
Slivered melon & prosciutto with Margarita (page 24)

APPETIZER
Burrata with beet & grated tomato (page 55)

INDEX

A

almonds: Asparagus with creamy almond tarator 49
Dukkah 193
Slivered melon & prosciutto 24
anchovies: Bitter leaf salad with lima beans & anchovy crumbs 70
Gilda pinxto 20
One-pot pasta e ceci 127
Seared beef tagliata with tonnato sauce 140
Stracciatella, anchovy & fried sage bruschetta 27
Anything goes clafoutis 170
artichokes: Artichoke & spinach lasagna bianca with panko crumbs 99
Artichoke, lemon & ricotta bruschetta 27
asparagus: Asparagus with creamy almond tarator 49
White asparagus vichyssoise 62
avocado: Fish taco party 148

B

Baked camembert board with dips 44
Baked feta with radishes, potato & harissa dressing 124
Baked saffron & pea risotto 116
Bake-to-order salty chocolate chip cookies 160
beef: Rotoli di bresaola 38
Seared beef tagliata with tonnato sauce 140
beets: Burrata with beet & grated tomato 55
Crispy gyoza salad with a zippy Thai-style dressing 52
berries: Anything goes clafoutis 170
Easy fruity jam tarts 182
Eton tower mess 173
Fudgy chocolate skillet cake 168
Macerated berry misù 179
Raspberry sorbet baked Alaska 176
Bitter leaf salad with lima beans & anchovy crumbs 70
Bloody Mary station 18
bread: Artichoke & spinach lasagna bianca with panko crumbs 99
Artichoke, lemon & ricotta bruschetta 27
Brioche pain perdu with mango fro-yo 180
Crostini 38
5-minute crispy rosemary & sea salt farinata 18
French onion soup for friends 138
Grated tomato "pan con tomate" bruschetta 26
Prosciutto grissini sticks 38
Stracciatella, anchovy & fried sage bruschetta 27
Whipped cod roe with pita chips & radishes 23
broccoli: Charred broccoli rabe with lemony cacio e pepe 87
Turmeric & coconut fish curry 151
Broiled chicken skewers with charred lettuce 75
Brothy wontons with crispy shallots & chili sauce 93
Brown butter cauliflower with polenta & scallops 143
butter: Spatchcock chicken with spiced butter sauce 134
Spiced butter eggs with lentils & crispy shallots 72
Butternut squash & sage tart with gorgonzola 121

C

cabbage: Broiled chicken skewers with charred lettuce 75
Crispy gyoza salad with a zippy Thai-style dressing 52
Fish taco party 148
Sweetheart cabbage with wild rice salad & raita 78
cannellini beans: Chicken-kinda cacciatore 128
Caramel-glazed duck legs with plums & endive 132
Caramelized shallot & radicchio bucatini 90
carrots: Crispy gyoza salad with a zippy Thai-style dressing 52
Make-ahead chicken stock 187
Spicy vermicelli noodle salad with crispy sausage 108
cauliflower: Brown butter cauliflower with polenta & scallops 143
celery: Make-ahead chicken stock 187
Lemony crunchy cucumber & celery salad 44
Charred broccoli rabe with lemony cacio e pepe 87
Cheat's miso-ramen noodle bowl with kimchi & greens 102
cheese: Artichoke & spinach lasagna bianca with panko crumbs 99
Artichoke, lemon & ricotta bruschetta 27
Baked feta with radishes, potato & harissa dressing 124
Burrata with beet & grated tomato 55
Butternut squash & sage tart with gorgonzola 121
Baked Camembert board with dips 44
Chile jam & blue cheese twists 34
Easy shrimp, tomato & feta orzo pasta 96
Figs with gorgonzola & salted maple pecans 31
Midweek 3-cheese & spinach skillet lasagna 100

Phyllo-fried feta with a tomato-caper salad 50
Salted caramel cheesecake pots 156
Spiced paneer & garbanzo beans in a cilantro broth 69
Stracciatella, anchovy & fried sage bruschetta 27
3-ingredient whipped feta dip 32
Tomato-mozzarella skewers 38
Watermelon, salted ricotta & mint salad 56
Wedge salad & blue cheese dressing 64
chicken: Broiled chicken skewers with charred lettuce 75
Chicken-kinda cacciatore 128
Make-ahead chicken stock 187
Spatchcock chicken with spiced butter sauce 134
chiles: Brothy wontons with crispy shallots & chili sauce 93
Chile jam & blue cheese twists 34
Homemade chili sauce 196
Lemongrass & cilantro paste 190
Sheet pan sea bass with fennel, potato & hot pepper flakes 112
Turmeric & ginger paste 190
chocolate: Bake-to-order salty chocolate chip cookies 160
Fudgy chocolate skillet cake 168
Pistachio & candied orange chocolate salame 165
coconut: One-pan roasted tomato, spinach & coconut dhal 122
Spiced paneer & garbanzo beans in a cilantro broth 69
cod roe: Whipped cod roe with pita chips & radishes 23
Confit tomato tarts with crispy sage 137
cranberries: Quick cranberry jam 45
Sweetheart cabbage with wild rice salad & raita 78
Creamy tortellini with pancetta, peas & leeks 88
Cremini mushroom, miso & lentil ragu 107
Crispy gyoza salad with a zippy Thai-style dressing 52
cucumber: Lemony crunchy cucumber & celery salad 44
Salmon with herby crème fraîche & salted cucumber 76
Smashed cucumber, sesame & cilantro salad 58
Virgin cucumber & mint mojito 23

D
drinks: Bloody Mary station 18
Fiery ginger & lemongrass iced tea 32
Get-ahead frozen margaritas 24
Grapefruit porto tonico 27
Hemingway daiquiri 20
Hibiscus cooler 34
Sage & citrus spritz 31
duck: Caramel-glazed duck legs with plums & endive 132
Dukkah 193
Dukkah-spiced schnitzel with herb & fennel salad 115

E
Easy fruity jam tarts 182
Easy shrimp, tomato & feta orzo pasta 96
eggplant: Glazed baby eggplant sticky rice bowls 152
eggs: Grapefruit crepes 162
Homemade meringue 198
Lemon aioli 188
Mayonnaise 188
Saffron aioli 188
Soy-cured eggs 102
Spiced butter eggs with lentils & crispy shallots 72
Eton tower mess 173
Everything bagel seasoning 193

F
fennel: Dukkah-spiced schnitzel with herb & fennel salad 115
Sheet pan sea bass with fennel, potato & hot pepper flakes 112
Fiery ginger & lemongrass iced tea 32
figs: Figs with gorgonzola & salted maple pecans 31
fish: Fish taco party 148
5-minute crispy rosemary & sea salt farinata 18
French onion soup for friends 138
fruit: Anything goes clafoutis 170
Eton tower mess 173
Fudgy chocolate skillet cake 168

G
garbanzo beans: One-pot miso, garbanzo, pancetta & kale stew 118
One-pot pasta e ceci 127
Spiced paneer & garbanzo beans in a cilantro broth 69
Get-ahead frozen margaritas 24
Gilda pinxto 20
ginger: Fiery ginger & lemongrass iced tea 32
Homemade chili sauce 196
Lemongrass & cilantro paste 190
Turmeric & ginger paste 190
Glazed baby eggplant sticky rice bowls 152
gnocchi: Skillet-fried gnocchi with wild mushrooms 82
grapefruit: Grapefruit crepes 162
Grapefruit porto tonico 27
Grated tomato "pan con tomate" bruschetta 26
gyoza: Brothy wontons with crispy shallots & chili sauce 93
Crispy gyoza salad with a zippy Thai-style dressing 52

H
hazelnuts: Dukkah 193
Sweetheart cabbage with wild rice salad & raita 78
Hemingway daiquiri 20
Hibiscus cooler 34
Homemade candied citrus peel 199
Homemade chili sauce 196
Homemade crispy shallots 197
Homemade meringue 198

J
jam: Easy fruity jam tarts 182

INDEX

K

kale: One-pot miso, garbanzo, pancetta & kale stew 118
kimchi: Cheat's miso-ramen noodle bowl with kimchi & greens 102

L

leeks: Creamy tortellini with pancetta, peas & leeks 88
lemon: Artichoke, lemon & ricotta bruschetta 27
  Charred broccoli rabe with lemony cacio e pepe 87
  Lemon aioli 188
  Lemon basil ricotta dumplings with blistered tomatoes 146
  Lemony crunchy cucumber & celery salad 44
  No-churn lemon meringue ice cream 159
  Rosé sgroppino 174
lemongrass: Fiery ginger & lemongrass iced tea 32
  Lemongrass & cilantro paste 190
  Spiced paneer & garbanzo beans in a cilantro broth 69
lentils: Cremini mushroom, miso & lentil ragu 107
  One-pan roasted tomato, spinach & coconut dhal 122
  Spiced butter eggs with lentils & crispy shallots 72
lettuce: Broiled chicken skewers with charred lettuce 75
  Wedge salad & blue cheese dressing 64
lima beans: Bitter leaf salad with lima beans & anchovy crumbs 70

M

Macerated berry misù 179
Make-ahead chicken stock 187
mango: Brioche pain perdu with mango fro-yo 180
Mayonnaise 188
Mediterranean mezze platter 39
melon: Slivered melon & prosciutto 24
meringue: Eton tower mess 173
  Homemade meringue 198
  No-churn lemon meringue ice cream 159
  Raspberry sorbet baked Alaska 176
Midweek 3-cheese & spinach skillet lasagna 100
miso: Cheat's miso-ramen noodle bowl with kimchi & greens 102
  Cremini mushroom, miso & lentil ragu 107
  One-pot miso, garbanzo, pancetta & kale stew 118
mushrooms: Cheat's miso-ramen noodle bowl with kimchi & greens 102
  Cremini mushroom, miso & lentil ragu 107
  Skillet-fried gnocchi with wild mushrooms 82
My favorite vinaigrette 194

N

No-churn lemon meringue ice cream 159
noodles: Cheat's miso-ramen noodle bowl with kimchi & greens 102
  Spicy vermicelli noodle salad with crispy sausage 108

O

olives: Chicken-kinda cacciatore 128
  Gilda pinxto 20
One-pan roasted tomato, spinach & coconut dhal 122
One-pot miso, garbanzo, pancetta & kale stew 118
One-pot pasta e ceci 127
onions: Brothy wontons with crispy shallots & chili sauce 93
  Everything bagel seasoning 193
  French onion soup for friends 138
  Homemade crispy shallots 197
  Spiced butter eggs with lentils & crispy shallots 72
oranges: Homemade candied citrus peel 199
  Pistachio & candied orange chocolate salame 165

P

pak choi: Brothy wontons with crispy shallots & chili sauce 93
  Cheat's miso-ramen noodle bowl with kimchi & greens 102
pasta: Artichoke & spinach lasagna bianca with panko crumbs 99
  Caramelized shallot & radicchio bucatini 90
  Charred broccoli rabe with lemony cacio e pepe 87
  Cremini mushroom, miso & lentil ragu 107
  Creamy tortellini with pancetta, peas & leeks 88
  Easy shrimp, tomato & feta orzo pasta 96
  Midweek 3-cheese & spinach skillet lasagna 100
  One-pot pasta e ceci 127
  Speedy Swed-ish weeknight meatballs 94
pecans: Figs with gorgonzola & salted maple pecans 31
peas: Baked saffron & pea risotto 116
  Creamy tortellini with pancetta, peas & leeks 88
pistachios: Pistachio & candied orange chocolate salame 165
plums: Caramel-glazed duck legs with plums & endive 132

polenta: Brown butter cauliflower with polenta & scallops 143
pork: Creamy tortellini with pancetta, peas & leeks 88
One-pot miso, garbanzo, pancetta & kale stew 118
Prosciutto grissini sticks 38
Spanish tomato soup with Serrano ham crisp 61
Slivered melon & prosciutto 24
Speedy Swed-ish weeknight meatballs 94
potatoes: Baked feta with radishes, potato & harissa dressing 124
Sheet pan sea bass with fennel, potato & hot pepper flakes 112
White asparagus vichyssoise 62

Q

Quick cranberry jam 45

R

radicchio: Bitter leaf salad with lima beans & anchovy crumbs 70
Caramelized shallot & radicchio bucatini 90
radishes: Baked feta with radishes, potato & harissa dressing 124
Whipped cod roe with pita chips & radishes 23
rice: Baked saffron & pea risotto 116
Glazed baby eggplant sticky rice bowls 152
Sweetheart cabbage with wild rice salad & raita 78
Rosé sgroppino 174

S

Saffron aioli 188
Sage & citrus spritz 31
salmon: Salmon with herby crème fraîche & salted cucumber 76
Wedge salad & blue cheese dressing 64
sausages: Speedy Swed-ish weeknight meatballs 94
Spicy vermicelli noodle salad with crispy sausage 108
sea bass: Sea bass acqua pazza with ancho chile 81
Sheet pan sea bass with fennel, potato & hot pepper flakes 112
Seared beef tagliata with tonnato sauce 140
seeds: Everything bagel seasoning 193
Smashed cucumber, sesame & cilantro salad 58
scallops: Brown butter cauliflower with polenta & scallops 143
shrimp: Easy shrimp, tomato & feta orzo pasta 96
Turmeric & coconut fish curry 151
Skillet-fried gnocchi with wild mushrooms 82
Slivered melon & prosciutto 24
Smashed cucumber, sesame & cilantro salad 58
Spanish tomato soup with Serrano ham crisp 61
Spatchcock chicken with spiced butter sauce 134
Speedy Swed-ish weeknight meatballs 94
Spiced butter eggs with lentils & crispy shallots 72
Spiced paneer & garbanzo beans in a cilantro broth 69
Spicy vermicelli noodle salad with crispy sausage 108
spinach: Artichoke & spinach lasagna bianca with panko crumbs 99
Midweek 3-cheese & spinach skillet lasagna 100
squash: Butternut squash & sage tart with gorgonzola 121
Sweetheart cabbage with wild rice salad & raita 78

T

The big sharing antipasto platter 38
3-ingredient whipped feta dip 32
tomatoes: Bloody Mary station 18
Burrata with beet & grated tomato 55
Chicken-kinda cacciatore 128
Confit tomato tarts with crispy sage 137
Easy shrimp, tomato & feta orzo pasta 96
Grated tomato "pan con tomate" bruschetta 26
Lemon basil dumplings with blistered tomatoes 146
One-pan roasted tomato, spinach & coconut dhal 122
Phyllo-fried feta with a tomato-caper salad 50
Sea bass acqua pazza with ancho chile 81
Spanish tomato soup with Serrano ham crisp 61
Tomato-mozzarella skewers 38
tuna: Seared beef tagliata with tonnato sauce 140
turmeric: Turmeric & ginger paste 190
Turmeric & coconut fish curry 151

V

Virgin cucumber & mint mojito 23

W

watermelon: Watermelon, salted ricotta & mint salad 56
Wedge salad & blue cheese dressing 64
Whipped cod roe with pita chips & radishes 23
White asparagus vichyssoise 62

Y

yogurt: Brioche pain perdu with mango fro-yo 180
Spiced butter eggs with lentils & crispy shallots 72
Sweetheart cabbage with wild rice salad & raita 78
3-ingredient whipped feta dip 32

ACKNOWLEDGMENTS

I'd like to say a huge thank you to everyone that helped bring this book to life. Thank you to Jenny Wapner, Catie Ziller, Carolyn Insley, and Kathy Steer on the editorial and Michelle Tilly, on the design. My heartfelt thanks go to my long-term creative collaborators Lisa Linder and Georgia Rudd, who I'm lucky enough to call both colleagues and friends. Huge thanks also to Sarah Vassallo, Rose Mordaunt, and Luke Churchill, who assisted on our long shoot days. Finally, thank you to my hugely supportive family, Mom, Dad, Robin, Benji, Alba, and Isla, who have the tough task of tasting all my experiments and the somewhat tougher task of dealing with the emotional roller coaster of book writing!

Hardie Grant North America
2912 Telegraph Ave
Berkeley, CA 94705
hardiegrantusa.com

Published in the United States by Hardie Grant North America, an imprint of Hardie Grant Publishing Pty Ltd.

Library of Congress Cataloging-in-Publication Data is available upon request
ISBN: 9781958417454
eBook ISBN: 9781958417461

Acquiring Editor: Catie Ziller
Photographer: Lisa Linder
Food and props styling: Frankie Unsworth
Styling assistants: Georgia Rudd and Sarah Vassallo
Designer: Michelle Tilly
Copy Editor: Kathy Steer

Printed in China

FIRST EDITION

Hardie Grant
NORTH AMERICA